Winning Hearts and Minds

Public Diplomacy in ASEAN

Edited by Sue-Ann Chia

**Singapore
International
Foundation**
for a better world

Distributed by

World Scientific Publishing Co. Pte. Ltd.
5 Toh Tuck Link, Singapore 596224
USA office: 27 Warren Street, Suite 401-402, Hackensack, NJ 07601
UK office: 57 Shelton Street, Covent Garden, London WC2H 9HE

Produced by

The Nutgraf
18 Howard Road
#06-06 Novelty BizCentre
Singapore 369585
www.nutgraf.com.sg

National Library Board, Singapore Cataloguing in Publication Data
Name(s): Chia, Sue-Ann, editor.
Title: Winning hearts and minds : public diplomacy in ASEAN / edited by Sue-Ann Chia.
Description: Singapore : The Nutgraf, [2022]
Identifier(s): ISBN 978-981-12-5043-9 (hardcover) | ISBN 978-981-12-5098-9 (paperback) |
    ISBN 978-981-12-5044-6 (ebook for institutions) |
    ISBN 978-981-12-5045-3 (ebook for individuals)
Subject(s): LCSH: Southeast Asia--Relations. | Southeast Asia--Foreign relations. |
    Cultural diplomacy--Southeast Asia.
Classification: DDC 327.59--dc23

British Library Cataloguing-in-Publication Data
A catalogue record for this book is available from the British Library.

For any available supplementary material, please visit
https://www.worldscientific.com/worldscibooks/10.1142/12671#t=suppl

Editorial Committee: Reuben Kwan, Singapore International Foundation
                      Lau Pei Hoon, Singapore International Foundation
                      Zhang Kangmin, Singapore International Foundation
                      Clifford Lee, The Nutgraf

Contents

Foreword

The shared history and sense of common destiny of the nations of the Association of Southeast Asian Nations (ASEAN) add a very meaningful layer to their people's identities. It is also why we strive to maintain peace and stability in our region, and to cooperate to unlock its tremendous potential for economic development. It is how ASEAN becomes larger than the sum of its parts, adding strength to each of its members, and enhancing its relevance amidst changing geopolitical tides.

The diplomacy of people must play an increasingly important role in the ASEAN project. Over the years, ASEAN countries have built up deeper working relations at the government-to-government level, with regular bilateral and multilateral exchanges. This traditional diplomacy between member states is necessary, but it is not near sufficient. We also need people to take a genuine interest in each other's cultures and way of life, and build up trust and understanding within the region.

The Singapore International Foundation (SIF) is deeply inserted in this work. It regularly creates opportunities for like-minded parties in the region to come together, share their knowledge, skills and resources and work on projects that are mutually beneficial. Their cultural exchange and volunteer cooperation programmes, and initiatives to connect young social entrepreneurs in the region, play a critical role in building people-to-people relationships.

To celebrate its 30th anniversary, the SIF has put together this collection of essays that captures the first-hand experiences of leading practitioners, stakeholders and researchers highlighting the development and practice of public diplomacy by ASEAN member states. The essays illustrate the many efforts at building ties - whether through exchanges that enrich mutual understanding of our varied circumstances and cultures and foster constructive dialogues, or a 'diplomacy of deeds' that make a real impact in the lives of local communities.

Our work in cultivating friendships is never done. The essays provide useful lessons on the intricacies of public diplomacy efforts, and more importantly, show us how we can do more to deepen collaboration in the region. We can look forward to the book inspiring more thinking and action around relationship-building, cooperative problem-solving and the building of a stronger common identity within ASEAN, to create a brighter future for us all.

Tharman Shanmugaratnam
Senior Minister and Coordinating Minister for Social Policies, Singapore

Introduction

In February 2020, the *MS Westerdam* faced a sudden crisis at sea. There were fears that someone on board the cruise ship, which was enroute to Japan from Hong Kong, had contracted the novel coronavirus that would eventually come to be known as COVID-19.

After Japan announced that the ship would not be allowed to dock at its ports, the Westerdam scrambled to find an alternative. But similar fears of the virus prompted four other countries to turn the ship away, leaving it to sail aimlessly for almost two weeks.

The situation grew desperate for the 2,257 people on board as the vessel ran out of fuel and food supplies. Then Cambodia came to the rescue. The country allowed the ship to dock in the coastal city of Sihanoukville so passengers could disembark, bringing an end to the saga. In its praise of the Southeast Asian nation, the World Health Organization lauded it as "a small country with a big heart".

This episode was one of the key points raised by Cambodian public policy analyst, Dr Chheang Vannarith, a contributor in this book. Despite the health risks, Cambodia's action was a boost to the country's image and a win for global solidarity. Its willingness to extend a helping hand has remained one of the few bright sparks in a dark period of human history.

Our world is currently seized with geopolitical tensions, plagued by a pandemic and filled with fake news that has divided individuals and countries alike. More recently, the rise of vaccine nationalism has highlighted how many governments are looking inward to solve the COVID-19 crisis. International relations seem to have faded into the background, and with it, a risk that trust will be eroded between nations.

But in this interconnected and globalised world, that is not the way forward. For countries to flourish, establishing strong trust and good relationships between governments, organisations and individuals is key. These are the building blocks of global collaboration and progression, as shown by Cambodia's gesture of goodwill and solidarity.

To build trust, however, we must recognise and understand each other's differences. This is why public diplomacy is now more important than ever. It is a more informal way for countries to communicate with the world – informing and influencing audiences overseas so as to advance foreign policy goals and improve international standing.

Public diplomacy, which some also associate with soft power, has been a dominant discourse in the United States and other developed countries. But it is not as established in Southeast Asia. This is rapidly changing as the region, among the most culturally and ethnically diverse in the world, steps up its public diplomacy campaign to charm the world.

Winning Hearts and Minds: Public Diplomacy in ASEAN explores how each Association of Southeast Asian Nations (ASEAN) nation has approached public diplomacy, which has evolved with changing times and technologies.

In Cambodia, Laos, Thailand and Vietnam, cultural diplomacy is considered an accessible and peaceful way of bridging peoples. Cultural exchanges can enrich mutual understanding, foster constructive dialogue and deepen relationships. More importantly, over time it will foster a sense of collective identity among the people of ASEAN.

In addition to cultural sharing, some ASEAN member states believe in the diplomacy of deeds. They engage in development cooperation or humanitarian aid to narrow development gaps and uplift their neighbours.

Also evident among many ASEAN member states is the ready acceptance of technology, particularly social media, as a powerful platform for interacting and engaging with audiences, both foreign and domestic. In the Philippines, for instance, the challenge is how to effectively engage with various publics in today's complex and democratised communications environment. Closer to home, Malaysia urges a rethink of public diplomacy and suggests three growth areas to explore, including "TechPlomacy".

Indeed, this is an interesting time for public diplomacy in ASEAN. As public diplomacy practice in the region gains momentum and depth, I hope this will pave the way for ASEAN member states to work together better while promoting our national interests.

Ambassador Ong Keng Yong
Chairman, Singapore International Foundation

About the Singapore International Foundation

The **Singapore International Foundation** makes friends for a better world.

We build enduring relationships between Singaporeans and world communities, harnessing these friendships to enrich lives and effect positive change.

Our work is anchored in the belief that cross-cultural interactions provide insights that strengthen understanding. These exchanges inspire action and enable collaborations for good.

Our programmes bring people together to share ideas, skills and resources in areas such as healthcare, education, arts and culture, as well as livelihood and business. We do this because we believe we all can, and should, do our part to build a better world, one we envision as peaceful, inclusive and offering opportunities for all.

Find out more at www.sif.org.sg

Singapore

"Public diplomacy ought to always be attentive to the historical legacy that social and emotional ties will always be privileged by target audiences over official political dealings. This is a dilemmatic strength as well as a weakness for Singapore's foreign policy."

Gardens by the Bay, Singapore

Singapore and Public Diplomacy

Alan Chong

As a modern political entity in international relations, Singapore had to be invented. It is a 55-year-old, *imagined* nation-state since it has by and large communicated its political, economic and social causes successfully (Chew, 1991). However, this creation of Singapore through the vigour of communication did not always emanate from a state. This much must be understood if one were to understand public diplomacy and its connections to Singaporean nationhood and statehood.

People Diplomacy Practices Pre-Independence (1954-64)

In its earliest modern origins under British colonialism, we find the predecessors of public diplomacy initiated by the foreign business community who had taken up residence in Singapore, which is basically a small island half the size of London as a city. British colonial immigration policies introduced to Singapore elements of ethnic groups who were not native to Southeast Asia. The arrival of Chinese and South Asian settlers in the fledgling colony brought into the local political equation significant elements of nationalist propaganda from China and India.

Singapore's original indigenous population was linked by blood ties to the Malay peoples of the Malay Peninsula and the islands of Indonesia. This added the strand of a Malay nationalism that emanated from just across the many narrow straits that surrounded Singapore. Along the way, discussion and support for Malay nationalism became intertwined with Islamic discourse from the Arab world and socialist ideas borrowed from the erstwhile Union of Soviet Socialist Republics (USSR) and Mao Zedong's communist party. The degrees of non-religious inspirations varied from one political party to another.

Public diplomacy is defined as "a government's process of communication with foreign publics in an attempt to bring about understanding of its nation's ideas and ideals, its institutions and culture, as well as its national goals and policies" (Hans Tuch, 1990). Those inspired by the proliferation of campaigns by the governments of Tony Blair, William J. Clinton, George W. Bush, Barack Obama and Xi Jinping coined even more additions to the lexicon of public diplomacy. Others suggest that public diplomacy is the product of a slick advertising campaign and a matter of making smart choices in "strategically targeting" foreign audiences to change their dispositions towards the governmental campaigner more positively (Fisher & Brockerhoff, 2008; Löffelholz, et al., 2014; Cull, 2019).

Still more polished examinations, including the elaborate, engineering-inspired *Soft Power 30* annual report that was temporarily suspended by the impact of the COVID-19 pandemic, suggest that any particular state's soft power could be measured by aggregating objective data like the attractiveness of government, digital infrastructure, national culture, engagement and enterprise, along with polling data on that particular state's image of friendliness, technological products, foreign policy, liveability, association with luxury goods, culture and even cuisine (McClory, 2020).

What is extremely pertinent in the case of Singapore is to understand that public diplomacy exists within a social context, and is usually cultivated over the long term through the mobilisation of intellectual and material resources. Singapore's experience with public diplomacy actually begins outside of statehood. To paraphrase Hans Tuch's definition earlier, nascent civil society back in the 1800s and 1900s attempted to communicate with foreign publics and governments in attempts to bring about understanding of its particular ideas and ideals, its institutions and culture, as well as direct their domiciled territories' goals and policies.

Public diplomacy is called into action because public opinion matters to the workings of government, regardless of whether it is democratic, authoritarian or totalitarian, or stripes in between, because it is a way of winnowing out diversity and contradictions in the people's voice. The latter is in turn an important pillar of legitimacy for whatever policies the governments of the day put out. Moreover, public opinion can support war, peace or austerity measures if guided to do so in the name of the public good *qua* national interest.

In mainstream political science, civil society is understood to be that portion of a nation-state where the government does not control (but can attempt to influence) its citizens and other transient persons who theoretically enjoy the liberal freedoms of rights to speech and expression, and especially, uncoerced association. In democratic theory, civil society acts in loose unison as a check against tyrannical turns in government policies. Civil society checks government by mounting its own syncretic versions of public diplomacy across all sorts of boundaries without necessarily representing any recognisable statehood. This is where one must appreciate why Singapore's experience with public diplomacy can be traced to vocal civil society groups of all ideological stripes and professions, including business entities. Of course, this may not be strictly public diplomacy by conventional measures, but agents of opinion becoming vocal across bureaucratic and political boundaries serve as the wellsprings of full-scale public diplomacy in the post-colonial era.

In sum, the period from the founding of the British Colony of Singapore to the eve of the Japanese Occupation in World War II revealed that significant non-state, almost diasporic, preliminary forms of public diplomacy were practised by the three main ethnic communities in Singapore. The thrust of these activities was aimed at pushing for political rights as much as they kept alive a sense of transborder political identity with the ancestral motherlands outside Singapore. This was to both prove nettlesome for an independent Singaporean statehood and a practised pathway for diasporic public diplomacy targeting Singapore's domestic politics.

There can be no perfect justification for compressing what some might argue to be the holistic drama of the Japanese Occupation cum World War II, the nationalistic propaganda that assisted constitutional and electoral agitation for independence from colonial rule, and the parallel communist-run revolutionary propaganda and civil disobedience campaign. In fact, one can possibly argue that the latter two played out concurrently with the Japanese Occupation. That said, this was a period of Singapore's political history that also witnessed considerable encounters with public diplomacy emanating from both state and non-state actors that responded to the attractive stakes that decolonisation entailed.

Ongoing Quest for a Niche Identity in the Global Economy (1965-Present)

Singapore's unexpected independence came on 9 August 1965. Right off the bat, Singapore wanted to keep its distinct identity as a non-aligned international trading hub open to all comers. Although this was the height of the Cold War, the government in Singapore did not wish to see ideology get in the way of uplifting its population through servicing Asia and the world at large in the re-export of goods, processing of mineral fuels, industrial raw materials, and the provision of financial services to multinational corporations and governments alike. Maoist China and Nehru's India were welcomed as trading partners even if their leaders did not openly favour Singapore's quasi-colonial "internal self-government" between 1955 and 1963.

Significantly, in Gretchen Liu's history of the Singapore Foreign Service, she recorded Foreign Minister S. Rajaratnam's open call in January 1964 for "a few politically skilled, roving ambassadors [to] be recruited for a diplomatic crusade in Asia, Africa and Latin America" (Liu, 2005).

Since then, Singapore's foreign policy has been almost synonymous with public diplomacy. Rajaratnam's landmark speech on Singapore's "omnidirectional" and ideologically-neutral foreign policy at the United Nations (UN) in 1965 continues to resonate in the way Singapore not only embraces the objectives of the Association of Southeast Asian

Nations (ASEAN) and the UN today, but also in its willingness to maintain communication channels and quietly productive economic relations with states that have rocky relations with the West such as Iran, North Korea and Myanmar (Chong & Ong-Webb, 2018).

Singapore's omnidirectional foreign policy also manifests in how it strives very hard to maintain even-handed relations with the United States and China and between China and Japan, China and India. The public diplomacy dimension of these balancing acts is manifest in the wide spectrum of special economic agreements and trade arrangements Singapore has signed with all of these major powers, while it also hosts substantive exchanges with government-linked think tanks based in these great powers. With ASEAN, there is also the added people-to-people dimension of fostering learning and exploratory exchanges amongst small- and medium-sized enterprises, schools and the respective civil service departments.

It is also a testimony of Singapore's formal public diplomacy sophistication that senior Ambassadors such as Tommy Koh, Kishore Mahbubani and Chan Heng Chee are often invited to semi-diplomatic colloquiums that involve the US and the EU. Ambassadors Barry Desker and K. Kesavapany are in turn closely associated with Singapore's permanent campaign to support economic multilateralism. Finally, Ambassador Ong Keng Yong is closely associated with supporting ASEAN, having served for a time as the regional body's Secretary-General.

It also helped that Singapore reinforced the people-to-people dimension of ties with ASEAN member populations through the award of ASEAN scholarships to non-Singaporean students to study in Singapore's prestigious universities and undertaking humanitarian assistance and disaster relief efforts in Indonesia's Aceh province, and the Leyte region in the Philippines between 2004 and 2013. Mass tourism and labour migration between Singapore and Brunei, Indonesia, Malaysia, the Philippines, Myanmar and Vietnam have also bolstered public diplomacy towards those countries despite the occasional ups and downs that arise from changes in government and leadership.

In many ways Singapore's many economic promotion agencies such as the Economic Development Board, Enterprise Singapore and the Ministry of Trade and Industry are all acting as entities engaged in public diplomacy whenever they attempt to "market" Singapore's hospitality to foreign investors in high technology companies and other sunrise industries such as biotechnology and robotics. The dedication shown by each official in these bodies to match foreign investors with local partners and other start-up firms reveals a human side to the economy that is quite unrivalled internationally. Singaporean "economic diplomats" are extremely enthusiastic about designing and co-investing in the best possible collaborative arrangements between foreign entities and local ones (Schein, 1996; Chong, 2014).

Today, Singapore's biggest challenge to its survival and prosperity is also a multidimensional one: globalisation of people on the move and economic activities transcending borders. The COVID-19 pandemic that struck the world between 2020 and 2021 has brought home both the fragility of globalisation's links and ironically, more than ever, the need to patch it back. Globalisation refers, of course, to the growing socio-economic interconnectedness of a worldwide capitalist economy that started with the expansion of European industrialisation into colonisation and trade since the 1800s (Waters, 2001). This in turn brought about unprecedented intercultural contact across hitherto geographically isolated peoples (Bauman, 1998).

In alternative geographies and histories, some scholars even argue that partial globalisations have occurred along the ancient Silk Roads across the Eurasian landmass, within the expanses of the erstwhile Roman Empire, and within what we term East Asia stretching from Japan, China and Korea down to Southeast Asia and South Asia (Frankopan, 2015; Chong & Ling, 2018). "Singapore Incorporated", along with nation-state Singapore, cannot remain an island in political imagination. It has to reprise its historical pathway since its invention in the 1800s as an entrepot of both goods and ideas, and increasingly intercultural understanding.

This is where the Singapore International Foundation (SIF) comes into its own as a focused practitioner of Singaporean public diplomacy. In its practice of "people diplomacy", it works with Singapore citizens – youth, academia, businesses and civil society, enabling collaboration with their overseas counterparts to effect positive change. It believes that "countries that bring their citizens into the fold and proactively engage the publics of another state in order to build mutual trust, respect and a shared future, have the edge. They tap into the growing influence wielded by non-state actors and, together with state-driven initiatives, enrich the tapestry of relations between nations" (Tan, 2017).

Parlaying compact Singapore's developmental expertise, the SIF is humbly extending bridges through its volunteer programmes in healthcare and education and good business initiatives in social entrepreneurship. The SIF also engages a diverse and talented group of artists to share Singapore's multiculturalism and contribute to positive social change through collaborations with international artists. Leveraging the power of digital media to connect communities and inspire collective actions globally, the SIF's digital storytelling initiative, *Our Better World*, aspires to harness digital disruption for social impact. The globalising world is still not yet one devoid of conflict, but at the very least Singapore's public diplomacy can transform an island-state of historical accidence into one of global possibilities through microcosmic demonstration of good governance while also learning about the island state's fragility through the eyes of others (George, 2001).

Conclusion

Singapore is stereotypically an *imagined* nation-state and mostly a product of colonial creation. Public diplomacy has served as its discursive fence. Although we have assumed that public diplomacy refers to "a government's process of communication with foreign publics in an attempt to bring about understanding of its nation's ideas and ideals, its institutions and culture, as well as its national goals and policies" (Tuch, 1990), it is quite clear that non-state public diplomacy has been especially pronounced at all stages of Singapore's political evolution. The very attempt at promoting each assorted non-state cause helps to shape the imagination of Singapore for its residents as well as the projection of its population's external orientations and kinship ties.

Put in another way, the non-state precedents of public diplomacy illuminate a structural tension. The thrust of these activities was aimed at pushing for political rights at home as much as they kept alive a sense of transborder political identity with the ancestral motherlands outside Singapore. This will act as a permanent handicap for an independent Singaporean statehood and a practised pathway for diasporic public diplomacy targeting Singapore's domestic politics. At the same time, the people-to-people dimension of linkages – whether one calls it public diplomacy, international relations or economic linkages, or social ties – will always be crucial to the way Singapore manages its soft power. Going forward, for organisations such as the SIF, public diplomacy ought to always be attentive to the historical legacy that social and emotional ties will always be privileged by target audiences over official political dealings. This is a dilemmatic strength as well as a weakness for Singapore's foreign policy.

Alan Chong

Alan Chong is Associate Professor and Head of the Centre for Multilateralism Studies at the S. Rajaratnam School of International Studies in Singapore. He has published widely on the notion of soft power and the role of ideas in constructing the international relations of Singapore and Asia.

References

Bauman, Z., 1998. *Globalization: The Human Consequences*. New York: Columbia University Press.

Chew, E., 1991. The Singapore National Identity: Its Historical Evolution and Emergence. In: E. C. Chew & E. Lee, eds. *A History of Singapore*. Singapore: Oxford University Press, pp. 357-368.

Chong, A., 2014. 'Global City Foreign Policy': The Propaganda of Enlargement and Integration of an IT-Connected Asian City. In: A. Chong & F. Yahya, eds. *State, Society and Information Technology in Asia: Alterity between Online and Offline Politics*. Farnham(Surrey): Ashgate Publishing, pp. 135-172.

Chong, A. & Ling, L., 2018. The Silk Roads: Globalization before Neoliberalization: Introduction to the special issue. *Asian Journal of Comparative Politics*, 3(3), pp. 189-193.

Chong, A. & Ong-Webb, G., 2018. Trump-Kim Summit: S. Rajaratnam and Singapore's Role. *RSIS Commentary CO18096*, 12 June.

Cull, N. J., 2019. *Public Diplomacy: Foundations for Global Engagement in the Digital Age*. Cambridge: Polity Press.

Fisher, A. & Brockerhoff, A., 2008. *Options for influence: Global campaigns of persuasion in the new worlds of public diplomacy*. London: Counterpoint - the cultural relations think-tank of the British Council.

Frankopan, P., 2015. *The Silk Roads: A New History of the World*. London: Bloomsbury Publishing.

George, C., 2001. Theme Parks, Business Parks and the Real Point of Contact. In: G. B. Lee, ed. *Singaporeans Exposed: Navigating the Ins and Outs of Globalisation*. Singapore: Landmark Books, pp. 33-37.

Liu, G., 2005. *The Singapore Foreign Service: The First 40 Years*. Singapore: Editions Didier Millet.

Löffelholz, M., Auer, C. & Srugies, A., 2014. Strategic Dimensions of Public Diplomacy. In: D. Holtzhausen & A. Zerfass, eds. *The Routledge Handbook of Strategic Communication*. Abingdon: Routledge, pp. 439-458.

McClory, J., 2020. *Soft Power 30. A Global Ranking of Soft Power 2019*. Washington DC: Portland.

Schein, E., 1996. *Strategic Pragmatism: The Culture of Singapore's Economic Development Board*. Cambridge(Massachusetts): The MIT Press.

Tan, J., 2017. Connecting and Collaborating to Change the World: Diplomacy in the Palms of Citizens. In: G. Koh, ed. *The Little Nation that Can. Singapore's Foreign Relations and Diplomacy*. Singapore: The National University of Singapore Society, pp. 150-158.

Tuch, H. W., 1990. *Communicating with the World: US Public Diplomacy Overseas*. New York: St Martin's Press.

Waters, M., 2001. *Globalization*. Second ed. Abingdon: Routledge

Brunei Darussalam

"For a small country like Brunei Darussalam with a population of under half a million, public diplomacy is all the more essential for us to enter the global public discussion and to be heard."

Masjid Omar Ali Saifuddien, Bandar Seri Begawan

A Bruneian Approach: Forging Friendships as Global Partners

Hafimi Abdul Haadii

For any country, public diplomacy is crucial and intrinsic to enabling understanding and building trust across borders, as well as raising the country's profile abroad. For a small country like Brunei Darussalam with a population of under half a million, public diplomacy is all the more essential for us to enter the global public discussion and to be heard.

While government initiatives are a major channel, public diplomacy takes place through unofficial routes too. Every citizen is an informal representative of our country. Even as we go out into the global sphere, we carry our values with us and must seek ways to respectfully express them in a foreign context.

As an entrepreneur, networking and forming connections are a part of my everyday life. In this, I am like many other citizens of Brunei Darussalam: constantly building connections and friendships with the rest of the world. Even as a small country, Brunei Darussalam has many avenues by which to extend its efforts in public diplomacy. We are a country and community that is always hospitable at home and ready to share about ourselves abroad.

Contributing to Global Peace and Prosperity

Regional groupings are one means by which a small country can still play a large role. The Association of Southeast Asian Nations (ASEAN) has long been a force for stability, and Brunei Darussalam is doing its part to uphold that purpose. As ASEAN Chair in 2021, and still under the constraints of COVID-19, Brunei Darussalam moved swiftly to mobilise the leaders of ASEAN member states and in response to incidents and challenges regionally and globally. Within the context of ASEAN, Brunei Darussalam has been very open about the strategies and deliverables during its ASEAN Chairmanship in 2021.

Brunei Darussalam convened an Informal ASEAN Ministerial Meeting via video conference as a consultative step to discuss and seek a consensus on the challenges facing ASEAN in 2021. This culminated in a statement that "called on all parties to refrain from instigating further violence, and for all sides to exercise utmost restraint as well as flexibility", while expressing "ASEAN's readiness to assist Myanmar in a positive, peaceful and constructive manner". Brunei Darussalam went on to call a special ASEAN Leaders' Meeting on 24 April, resulting in a five-point consensus plan to de-escalate the situation. As ASEAN Chair, Brunei Darussalam continues to shoulder the responsibility of helping the region navigate this current crisis as a fair and neutral Chair.

As a responsible global citizen, Brunei Darussalam is working towards the United Nations' (UN) Sustainable Development Goals (SDGs). In 2020, the country submitted its first ever voluntary national review on its progress towards the SDGs, at the UN's High-Level Political Forum on Sustainable Development. In the review, we shared the best practices, lessons learned and challenges encountered in our SDG journey, in the hope that these may be useful for other countries on the same path. We also laid out our Whole-of-Nation approach, in which local not-for-profit organisations and the private sector enter into a partnership with the government to contribute to this national effort. The report is simply part of Brunei Darussalam's larger participation in this global effort. We take part in meetings and workshops, organised by the UN and ASEAN, to promote cooperation and capacity building, as well as to share our best practices in working towards the goals.

One regional effort through which Brunei Darussalam has aimed to build human capacity and strengthen ties is the Brunei-US English Language Enrichment Project for ASEAN. Launched in 2012, the US$25 million project has sent instructors across the region to teach English to diplomats and officials. The project not only furthers Brunei Darussalam's public diplomacy efforts, but also improves the diplomatic landscape of the region through this capability building.

Cultural Diplomacy

Brunei Darussalam has a rich cultural heritage and like many countries is supportive of cultural diplomacy as a peaceful and accessible way to strengthen global friendships and long term trust. At the government level, Brunei Darussalam engages with other countries through the sharing of arts, culture and heritage. In 2018, for instance, Bandar Seri Begawan played host to a month-long series of cultural exchange activities with China, including an exhibition on Silk Road cultures, seminars and performances. The COVID-19 pandemic has not hampered the continued deepening of cultural ties, with Brunei Darussalam marking the Brunei-China Year of Tourism 2020 with a cultural carnival in the capital at the end of the year.

Besides promoting understanding, Brunei Darussalam also works to jointly build capacity with others in the area of culture. The Titian Budaya Malaysia-Brunei Darussalam programme in 2010 drew upon similarities between both nations, opening avenues for cooperation and collaboration in areas such as joint training in arts and cultural fields; the exchange of materials between national libraries; collaborative research on traditional performances, craft and customs, in the context of both nations' shared Malay heritage; and the exchange of broadcast documentaries.

Cultural exchange happens at the community level as well, in a less formal version of cultural diplomacy, as arts groups make connections with their counterparts elsewhere. In 2018, the Brunei Art Forum signed a memorandum of understanding with the Korean Fine Arts Association, paving the way for cultural exchange and collaboration between the artists of both countries. Cultural dialogues are a way for Brunei Darussalam to learn about itself through the eyes of others, too. In December 2020, for instance, the diplomatic corps held a photo exhibition titled "Brunei Darussalam from the Eyes of Foreign Diplomats and their Families". Featuring photographs of Brunei Darussalam captured by heads of missions, their staff and families, the exhibition offered a glimpse into how Brunei Darussalam is perceived by its foreign friends.

Diaspora Diplomacy and People-to-People Ties
Some diplomatic efforts take place right at home. Brunei Darussalam plays

host to many foreign expatriates, from countries such as Australia, the United Kingdom, South Korea, Japan and India, to those closer to home: Malaysia, Singapore, Indonesia, the Philippines, Thailand, Cambodia and Vietnam. Many of them have lived in Brunei Darussalam for more than two decades, becoming an enduring part of the country's societal landscape and forming ties within the community. Informal cultural exchanges happen every day at this people-to-people level. These organically-formed relationships could yield rich dividends, whether intangible in the form of goodwill and understanding or tangible examples such as business networks and overseas contacts.

Abroad, Bruneian youth are the country's best source of citizen ambassadors. Brunei Darussalam has strong academic ties with countries such as Singapore, Malaysia, Australia, the United Kingdom and the United States. When studying abroad, many young Bruneians are informal ambassadors of our country, sharing about Bruneian culture with those they meet and forging friendships with others worldwide.

Brunei Darussalam has long built relationships with the international community through educational programmes, international scholarships, and youth exchanges. Through such programmes, participants gain an understanding of different nations. Besides reinforcing their appreciation of their own community and country, they also learn to be open to different ways of life. Such youth programmes and exchanges are also a core part of public diplomacy efforts, establishing relationships that could become vital in later decades. One might imagine, for instance, future leaders of countries meeting at a very early stage of their lives and laying the foundations for deeper personal and professional trust when they rise to other positions in their careers.

Homegrown social enterprises and volunteer groups, too, can share Brunei Darussalam's culture and values with the world when they take Bruneian youth volunteers across the region to help the less fortunate. One example is Hand4handbn, which has done volunteer work in Brunei Darussalam, Cambodia, Indonesia, Malaysia and Bangladesh, from building homes to distributing food. Its strategy is to work with local non-governmental organisations in the host country, thus forming ties with counterparts on the ground and being more thoroughly embedded in the country's volunteer ecosystem.

The ASEAN Young Professionals Volunteer Corps which was initiated by Brunei Darussalam in 2013, ran for three years, sending volunteer professionals from each of the ASEAN member states to partake in community building efforts through two-week assignments in Indonesia, Cambodia, the Philippines, Laos, Vietnam and Myanmar. This helped to foster networking opportunities amongst the ASEAN young professionals from various sectors, which would assist them in their future career paths. Another initiative is the Singapore-Brunei Youth Leaders Exchange Program (SBYLEP), a joint effort between Brunei Darussalam and Singapore, which saw the exchange of potential youth leaders from both countries that has been ongoing since 2014.

And then there are business groups and events that were initiated by Brunei Darussalam entrepreneurs such as the ASEAN-China Young Entrepreneurs Forum and ASEAN Young Entrepreneurs Council. Brunei Darussalam was also honoured to have hosted the 5th ASEAN-China Young Entrepreneurs Forum in 2013, which brought together 200 young entrepreneurs from ASEAN and China, to establish business-to-business linkages and exchange insights on shaping the future of our respective countries' economies. But business links were, of course, not the only ties that were forged. Beyond gaining a deeper understanding of our economies, we also formed personal connections.

As an entrepreneur, I have found that supportive networking is central to success. Even from an early stage of our lives, the connections that bind and the relationships built span over a lifetime. In public diplomacy, the same applies. By weaving both these formal and informal connections across the world, Brunei Darussalam and its citizens can build strong and reliable international networks, which can be counted upon in challenging times.

Hafimi Abdul Haadii

Hafimi Abdul Haadii is currently Executive Director of LVK Group of Companies. She is also an appointed Member of the Legislative Council of Brunei Darussalam since 2017 and is the Chairperson of Competition Commission of Brunei Darussalam since 2018.

Cambodia

"(Cambodia's) public diplomacy is also in transition from a propaganda machine to a tool for public communication and engagement. In other words, it brings the public dimension to diplomacy."

Independence Monument, Phnom Penh

Cambodia's Changing Public Diplomacy and Nation Branding

Chheang Vannarith

C ambodia is transitioning to modern diplomacy by integrating economic and cultural diplomacy into its traditional diplomacy, which focuses on peace, security, national sovereignty and independence. The Economic Diplomacy Strategy (2021-2023), launched in early 2021, intends to coordinate government agencies and build capacity for Cambodian diplomats and relevant stakeholders to promote trade, investment and tourism. Economic diplomacy is also aimed at diversifying economic partners and the sources of growth.

Overall, the country's public diplomacy is also in transition from a propaganda machine to a tool for public communication and engagement. In other words, it brings the public dimension to diplomacy. But it has been practised on an ad hoc basis, without systematic thinking and design. Hence, it remains largely reactive and fragmented, and the public diplomacy capacity of Cambodian diplomats is still limited. Although the strategic narratives have been enhanced over the past few years, there is still room for improvement.

The key narratives being developed at the moment are:

- Cambodia is an independent and sovereign state to counter the narrative that it is a vassal state or Trojan horse of China.
- Cambodia is a responsible ASEAN member to counter the narrative that it is the spoiler of ASEAN unity.
- Cambodia is a democratic country to counter the narrative that it is an authoritarian regime or even a dictatorship.

In general, from the Cambodian perspective, public diplomacy's roles are to shape public opinion, raise national prestige and status, and promote international persuasion power. Public diplomacy functions include:

- Providing inputs to foreign policy formation
- Reaching out to the public
- Engaging various stakeholders
- Developing narratives to envision the future

Both traditional and social media platforms have been actively used to share information and convey official messages, especially when defending and explaining Cambodia's position on national and international issues. However, the number of viewers of the social media platforms of the Ministry of Foreign Affairs and International Cooperation remains relatively low. To boost online engagement, digital diplomacy – the use of digital platforms to advance Cambodia's public diplomacy – is being developed.

Currently, Cambodia's public diplomacy consists of three pillars: cultural diplomacy, peace diplomacy and humanitarian assistance.

All three are held up by the core values of inclusivity and open multilateralism. Prime Minister Hun Sen stated at the high-level meeting to commemorate the 75th Anniversary of the United Nations on 21 September 2020: "Cambodia recognises the central role of multilateralism in addressing complex global challenges we face today. Our challenges are interconnected and can only be addressed through reinvigorated multilateralism." This was reiterated by Foreign Minister Prak Sokhonn who said: "Cambodia's foreign policy is firmly underpinned by a strong spirit of multilateralism."

Cultural Diplomacy

Rich in historical and cultural heritage, Cambodia has advantages and assets to project its international image and prestige through cultural cooperation and engagement. It aspires to become the cultural gateway of the Mekong region, and is able to share several success stories of international cooperation on preserving and safeguarding its heritage sites with other countries.

Among them is the International Coordinating Committee for the Safeguarding and Development of the Historic Site of Angkor (ICC-Angkor), which has become the international cooperation model on safeguarding World Heritage Sites with the support of the United Nations Educational, Scientific and Cultural Organization (UNESCO). France and Japan are the co-chairs of ICC-Angkor, which was formed in 1993 at the Intergovernmental Conference on the Safeguarding and Development of the Historic Site of Angkor. In 2003, the second Intergovernmental Conference was held in Paris, and the Paris Declaration was released to reaffirm the international commitment and coordination to safeguard and properly develop the Angkor site.

Another example is the Preah Vihear temple. When the ancient Hindu temple was registered as a World Heritage Site in 2008, the International Coordinating Committee for Safeguarding and the Development of Preah Vihear (ICC-Preah Vihear) was created in 2014 with support from UNESCO. China and India are the co-chairs of the ICC-Preah Vihear. From 2013 to 2016, the World Heritage Fund provided support to consolidate and improve the monument's structural stability. In 2018, the United States provided financial support to restore the monument's northern staircase under the Ambassadors Fund.

Cultural exchanges have also been promoted with the setting up of the Asian Cultural Council (ACC) in January 2019. Formed under the institutional umbrella of the International Conference of Asian Political Parties (ICAPP), the ACC aims to promote cultural exchanges and heritage preservation, and connect culture with peace, sustainable development and innovation. The secretariat of the ACC is located in the Cambodian capital of Phnom Penh.

Gastrodiplomacy – the promotion of Khmer cuisine abroad – is also gaining traction. Cambodian diplomats and their spouses must take a cooking class before their posting to overseas missions. A cooking book has been printed for distribution among the diplomatic community. Titled *The Taste of Angkor*, it was published by the Ministry of Foreign Affairs and International Cooperation to further promote Khmer cuisine overseas.

Peace Diplomacy

As a post-conflict country, Cambodia has vast experience in peace-building. The Win-Win policy leading to the end of the civil war in December 1998 has been promoted at home and abroad. At the

ASEAN-related meetings in 2012, Cambodia's Ministry of National Defence distributed the book on Prime Minister Hun Sen's Win-Win policy to regional participants to promote international awareness and knowledge sharing on conflict resolution in Cambodia. In 2020, the Ministry of Foreign Affairs and International Cooperation developed a concept proposal on policy dialogue and public research on the policy.

With support from the United Nations (UN) and development partners, Cambodia has transformed from a recipient to a sending country of peacekeeping forces. Since 2006, Cambodia has sent more than 7,000 peacekeepers, of whom more than 400 are women, to partake in the UN peacekeeping operations (PKO) in nine war-torn countries. Notably, Cambodia is ranked number 17 out of 120 countries that dispatch women to the UN PKO. Among the ASEAN member states, as of December 2020, Cambodia was ranked third on women participation in the UN PKO (after Indonesia and Malaysia). Cambodia also promotes the roles of women in peacekeeping operations.

Moreover, as a country with one of the world's highest landmine casualty rates, Cambodia has become a strong international advocate of the campaign to ban anti-personnel landmines and shares its expertise in landmine clearance. In 2012, as the Chair of ASEAN, Cambodia proposed establishing the ASEAN Regional Mine Action Centre (ARMAC). This aims to enhance awareness programmes on the danger of explosive remnants of war (ERW) among the affected communities, facilitate appropriate medical and rehabilitation assistance for victims of ERW upon request from affected ASEAN member states, and assist interested ASEAN countries in research and knowledge sharing on the effects of EWR and efforts to address them.

In 2016, the headquarters of ARMAC was inaugurated in Cambodia, and the secretariat of ARMAC was formed in 2017. The Steering Committee members are ambassadors of ASEAN member states to Cambodia, and the chair of the committee is rotated among the member states in alphabetical order.

Humanitarian Assistance

Cambodia has been lauded as "a small country with a big heart" by the World Health Organization (WHO) after it permitted the *MS Westerdam* cruise ship to dock at its Sihanoukville seaport on 13 February 2020. A day later, on Valentine's Day, the Prime Minister went to welcome the first batch of disembarked passengers with a rose. The cruise ship had spent nearly two weeks at sea after being turned away by multiple ports over fears that passengers onboard carried the COVID-19 virus. With support from the WHO and technical partners, Cambodia safely managed the public health risks of receiving the *MS Westerdam*. The WHO's statement issued on 25 June 2020 read: "Cambodia's response to the *MS Westerdam* crisis demonstrates that a country with fewer resources can contribute to global health security. It can take a humanitarian approach in a public health crisis and deliver a measured, coordinated response despite the uncertainty and complex challenges."

Cambodia also provided seven million face masks and other medical supplies to Laos, Myanmar, Timor-Leste and Nepal from late 2020 to early 2021 as part of international efforts to fight the COVID-19 pandemic. The gestures demonstrate Cambodia's goodwill diplomacy and humanitarian action to support others during difficult times to promote global efforts and solidarity.

Challenges Ahead

Cambodia's public diplomacy is still at a nascent stage. Investments in training and skill development programmes are needed to advance its national interests through public diplomacy and nation branding. Narratives and deeds must be consistent, as consistency is critical in building trust.

Cambodia is facing widespread negative narratives magnified by certain media outlets and think tank communities, especially concerning reports that it is a client state or vassal state of China. It is an uphill struggle for Cambodia to convince sceptics that the country is not a vassal state to China or any other major powers. Building an independent nation is part of the nation branding process.

Chheang Vannarith

Chheang Vannarith is a public policy analyst and government relations strategist. He has over a decade of research experience in geopolitical and political economic analysis, with a focus on Southeast Asia. He is the President of the Asian Vision Institute.

Indonesia

"*The landscape and tools of public diplomacy have changed substantially. To succeed, the government has to adapt to the public preference, not the other way around. For better or worse, optics have become much more important in foreign policy, and by extension, public diplomacy. There is a risk, however, that emphasising optics over substance may not always be healthy for diplomacy.*"

Borobudur Temple, Java

Indonesia's Public Diplomacy: The Growing Role of Optics in Foreign Policy

Dino Patti Djalal

In Indonesia's foreign policy, some things remain the same while others change. I would say that the one thing that has changed the most is in the realm of public diplomacy. The attention to optics in the execution of Indonesia's foreign policy today is arguably the highest ever.

In the ultra-competitive public information space, how policy-makers are seen is as important as, if not more important than, the substance of the policy itself. This, of course, is but the latest trend of long-standing efforts to garner public support for foreign policy.

Indonesia's first President, Soekarno, eager to project Indonesia as a leader of the world's "new emerging forces", used massive public rallies to drum up support for his revolutionary foreign policy projects. Political propaganda and indoctrination – against "neo-imperialists and neo-colonialists" – were commonly used to mobilise the masses.

This method of public rallies was abandoned by his successor, President Suharto, who pursued a low-key foreign policy run by diplomats who preferred to work behind closed doors, avoiding the media spotlight and contact with the public. Foreign policy was not a legitimising factor to the Government, so it was not necessary to please the domestic audience at home with public diplomacy.

Public diplomacy assumed greater importance in the 1980s. A key reason was the increasingly negative exposure Indonesia was facing from the Western media and non-governmental organisations (NGOs) on issues such as human rights and the situation in East Timor. This prompted Foreign Minister Mochtar Kusumaatmadja to initiate what he called "cultural diplomacy", which was intended to show the world that Indonesia was a civilised nation with rich cultures and not a cruel one as had been portrayed by some of its critics. The target audience was the international community, not the public in Indonesia. This cultural diplomacy was, however, short-lived due to lack of funding and management.

It was Foreign Minister Ali Alatas who, in the 1990s, intensified public diplomacy by the Department of Foreign Affairs. This task was spearheaded by the Directorate-General for Social and Cultural Affairs and Information, who organised an information campaign to deflect political and media attacks against Indonesia from foreign entities. While the target audiences of this campaign were those residing outside the country, more attention was also paid to the domestic audience. Foreign Minister Alatas deemed it necessary to raise public awareness – and thus support – for the country's foreign policy issues.

Rebuilding an International Image

By this time, the Indonesian public had become increasingly exposed to external pressures, mainly from Western governments and media, on the country's human rights issues. There were alarming signs that public opinion was turning against the government.

On East Timor, for instance, the shooting of hundreds of protesters at Santa Cruz (1991), the Nobel Peace Prize award to East Timorese Bishop Carlos Belo and politician Jose Ramos Horta (1996), the massive violence and chaos which followed the 1999 referendum and the brutal killing of three United Nations (UN) staff members by pro-Indonesia Timorese militias in Atambua (2000) all gave Indonesia a serious black eye and damaged its international reputation.

All this mattered because if there is one constant for successive Indonesian governments, it is the desire for a good international image. There is something about the Indonesian psychology which yearns for recognition and respectability. For proud Indonesians, there is nothing they dislike more than to be portrayed as an international pariah or outcast. Eventually, Indonesia's public diplomacy shifted from damage control to image building in the *"reformasi"* era (reformation), which began after the fall of President Suharto in 1998 during the financial crisis and set in motion Indonesia's democratic transition.

Despite a myriad of initial post-crisis problems during this period of reformation, Indonesia has gradually rebounded since the term of fifth President Megawati Soekarnoputri who was in power from 2001 to 2004. The economy recovered, the security situation improved and political stability returned. The Indonesian government slowly regained its confidence, domestically and internationally. One foreign analyst wrote that Indonesia had returned as a "normal country".

President Susilo Bambang Yudhoyono, who assumed office in 2004 and was, by all measures, a foreign policy President, began to reposition Indonesia in international affairs, and also further reframed the country's image. Both to international and domestic audiences, the Yudhoyono administration began to promote new foreign policy narratives: Indonesia as the world's third largest democracy (which became an important connecting point with the West); the country with the world's largest Muslim population (a relevant theme in the post-9/11 world); the largest country and economy in Southeast Asia (to underscore Indonesia's geopolitical significance).

In this light, public diplomacy gained more substance. The government initiated the Presidential Visitors Program, where special "friends of Indonesia" from key countries were invited – all expenses paid – to Independence Day celebrations at the Presidential Palace. Foreign Minister Hassan Wirajudha routinely organised "foreign policy breakfasts", where he would invite public figures and opinion leaders to brief them on specific foreign policy issues.

The Foreign Ministry appointed an effective spokesperson – Marty Natalegawa who later became Foreign Minister. He was well-informed on diplomatic issues, gave weekly press briefings and was available to the media round the clock. (Prior to this, the role of spokesperson in the Foreign Ministry was somewhat non-existent). Marty became an instant public hit.

The government also began to court Indonesian diasporas in an effort to secure their participation in national development. There are around six million Indonesians overseas, a large support base to tap on.

Today, the importance of public diplomacy has increased significantly. Two factors have led to this development.

New Media, New Ways to Appeal to Audiences
The first is the dynamics of Indonesian democracy and the ever-changing information landscape. In the last decade, the public information space has become extremely competitive. Unlike in the old days, government officials are no longer guaranteed a spot on the front page – indeed, there are plenty of ministers who, despite their good work, seldom get media coverage.

Meanwhile, the Indonesian public has become much more demanding, more knowing, more vocal and more critical than ever before. This leads to an environment where the performance of policy-makers is often judged by his/her public visibility. For better or worse, this turns the already difficult job of governing into a fierce popularity contest, where ministers would compete for media and public attention.

The other factor is the emergence of social media, which has dominated the way people get their daily dose of information. There is no doubt that social media has become a game-changer. Social media has reaffirmed to policy-makers that there is a large audience of information-seekers out there for the taking and, more importantly, they could be reached directly – and also easily and freely – without the need for media reporters as conventional intermediaries. Using social media, policy-makers feel they can inform the public as often as they like, and as much or as little as they wish. From the comments, likes and retweets, they can also get direct responses and gauge public opinion.

Social media, however, requires a different approach from conventional media. To attract a large audience, the messaging has to be short and simple, not long and complicated. Technocratic jargon and high-sounding phrases would not gain attention. There is no room for lengthy analysis. Many people also like to see photos before they read words, which explains why Instagram is more popular than Twitter in Indonesia. The use of humour to convey a point is also highly recommended. Policy-makers and politicians suddenly find themselves having to adapt their way of public messaging – and not everyone is managing.

Foreign Minister Retno Marsudi, however, is a notable exception. She is not only the first woman to be named Foreign Minister, but is also the first Indonesian Foreign Minister to rely heavily on social media. It is worth noting that Retno assumed office at a time when foreign policy had little constituency, and she was serving President Joko Widodo, who was very popular but showed marginal interest in foreign policy. At this juncture, an important objective for Indonesian public diplomacy therefore was how foreign policy undertakings could help bolster public attention at home. But this became a challenging task.

At first, the foreign policy establishment struggled to get President Joko's attention. They needed to prove to the leader, who in those early days did not enjoy going to international summits, that foreign policy would bring direct and tangible benefits for domestic needs.

Eventually, two particular issues stood out which connected foreign policy and domestic politics.

The first was the protection of Indonesian citizens abroad, especially workers. There are about two million Indonesian workers who send sizeable remittances to their families back home, and any mishaps that befall them usually capture public attention and become a political issue. The second were issues relating to the Islamic world – Palestine, Rohingya, Afghanistan, relations with Saudi Arabia, Organisation of Islamic Cooperation, the cartoon of Prophet Muhammad – all of which resonated strongly with the Islamic constituents and boosted President Joko's position in the run-up to the 2019 elections.

As President Joko was enormously popular with netizens, social media strategy was systematically built into the work of Foreign Minister Retno. She would attend conferences and events with a social media team, and every activity would be beamed to Instagram and Twitter followers.

Foreign Ministry events would often invite influencers and celebrities with large followings. Editors would get calls to retweet or post the last tweets of the Foreign Minister. Getting hits, retweets and likes became an important metric for public diplomacy. As a policy tool, the wide reach of social media also conveniently compensates for the small budget – less than US$2 million – allocated to the Directorate for Public Diplomacy. The use of social media has also led to noticeable efforts to impress the youth, especially the millennials, who made up large social segments that became critical in the 2019 elections.

Over time, the style of Indonesian public diplomacy has evolved. Similar to how social media has changed how politicians communicate online to domestic and foreign audiences, offline events have also been impacted.

Indonesia's annual Year End Press Statement – an important tradition in the Department of Foreign Affairs – used to be a typical diplomatic event, where guests come to listen to the Foreign Minister's thoughts and plans. In recent years, it has become a glitzy show with fancy PowerPoint presentations, songs, performances and theatrical lights.

In conclusion, the landscape and tools of public diplomacy have changed substantially. To succeed, the government has to adapt to the public preference, not the other way around. For better or worse, optics have become much more important in foreign policy, and by extension, public diplomacy. There is a risk, however, that emphasising optics over substance may not always be healthy for diplomacy.

Dino Patti Djalal

Dino Patti Djalal is Founder of the Foreign Policy Community of Indonesia. He is a distinguished career diplomat, having served in Indonesia's missions in London, Dili and Washington D.C. He was Presidential Spokesperson and Foreign Policy Advisor (2004-2010), Ambassador of Indonesia to the United States (2010-2013) and Vice Minister for Foreign Affairs (2014).

Laos

"Laos has come a long way. Both the government and civil society are making conscious efforts to project a more balanced image of the country as independent, capable and boasting unique charms."

Wat Mixay, Vientiane

From Spectator to Player: Laos' Diplomacy and Cultural Engagement

Anoulak Kittikhoun
Aditta Kittikhoun

This essay discusses Laos' diplomacy and engagement in the international arena, with a focus on the Association of Southeast Asian Nations (ASEAN), the premier regional cooperation body. Drawing on the upcoming book, *Small Countries, Big Diplomacy: Laos at the UN, ASEAN and MRC* (Kittikhoun & Kittikhoun, 2021 in press), the first part of the essay deals with the role of Laos during its chairmanship of ASEAN in 2016, in which the country made efforts to facilitate and broker agreements among ASEAN members and the great powers on the South China Sea – a highly sensitive and contentious issue of global concern.

The second half deals with efforts by the government and other actors in the tourism, entertainment, media and cultural sectors. Both efforts are concerned with the international image and (mis)perception, or lack thereof, of Laos in the world and aim to promote a more balanced understanding of the country.

High Drama and Quiet Diplomacy: Laos' Leadership in ASEAN

Laos emerged from a great Southeast Asian civilisation along the mighty Mekong River and has been subjected to regional and external conflagrations and wars. It also endured the heaviest aerial bombardment in the history of humankind. Indeed, it has not been easy for Laos, landlocked and surrounded by five bigger neighbours, to find its place in the world.

In the post-Cold War era, Laos, along with Vietnam, Myanmar and Cambodia, joined ASEAN, embracing its goals to bring about development and trade benefits, as well as regional integration and connectivity. There were two major moments of international diplomacy for Laos on the ASEAN stage – the chairmanship in 2004 and in 2016.

The 10th ASEAN Summit in Vientiane in 2004 produced the Vientiane Action Programme (VAP). The six-year plan aimed to deepen regional integration and narrow the development gap within ASEAN. There were other important political milestones reached at the Vientiane Summit. First, it was in the VAP that the member states agreed to work towards the ASEAN Charter – the legally binding document that has formally governed ASEAN relations since 2007. Second, ASEAN leaders agreed to hold the first East Asia Summit (EAS) the following year in Malaysia – a political victory for ASEAN-led regional security. Third, the leaders also adopted for the first time the "ASEAN Security Community" blueprint to complement the "ASEAN Economic Community" initiative.

While the summit did achieve concrete results, there was also no particular issue that divided the region. Yet the 2004 Summit was of special symbolic importance for Laos. In the words of academic Vatthana Pholsena, "it was no small achievement" for "a country that joined the organisation less than 10 years ago [to chair the group] after decades of war followed by several years of diplomatic and economic ostracism from the international community" (Pholsena, 2005).

Things were vastly different when Laos took the chair again in 2016. The biggest international political, peace and security issue facing ASEAN and the region at the time was the South China Sea dispute. What was (and is) at stake were global trade benefits (estimated to be worth US$5 trillion, or over one-third of the annual global trade flow) and territorial control of areas rich in not only fish stocks but also oil and natural gas (up to 17.7 billion tons of crude oil).

The issue mainly involves China and four countries in ASEAN, namely Brunei, Malaysia, the Philippines, and Vietnam. The United States, a non-claimant state, is also highly invested in the issue due to significant trade, political and security interests in the region. In 2012, at the ASEAN Foreign Ministers' Meeting (AMM) in Phnom Penh chaired by Cambodia, ASEAN did not issue a joint communique for the first time in its 45-year history, mainly due to disagreements over the South China Sea issue.

Adding to the tension, the Philippines in 2013 lodged a case against China in the Permanent Court of Arbitration (PCA) in the Hague, stating it violated the United Nations Convention on the Law of the Sea (UNCLOS). While the PCA stated clearly on 12 July 2016 that it did not "rule on any question of sovereignty over land territory and does not delimit any boundary between the Parties" (Permanent Court of

Arbitration, 2016), it agreed with the Philippines, concluding that there was "no legal basis for China to claim historic rights" over its demarcation lines in the contested territories. The US and other Western nations called on China to accept the ruling. China, which did not participate in the arbitration, rejected the verdict.

With such high stakes, pressure mounted and all eyes were on Laos to see how it would handle the issue at the ASEAN Summit that year. Laos was determined to approach the issue with clear principles, patience and even-handedness. Laos is a friend of China but it is also friends with Vietnam and other ASEAN states. A believer in ASEAN centrality, unity, and objectives, Laos resolved to adhere to the theme of the 2016 Summit: "Turning Vision into Reality for a Dynamic ASEAN Community".

The first test was the AMM on 24 July 2016, which was supposed to issue a joint communique on various issues and initiatives. An earlier Senior Officials' Meeting (SOM) already witnessed divisions over the South China Sea dispute that had grown even more pronounced. The Philippines was pushing for some recognition of the recent ruling by the PCA. This was supported by Vietnam, Malaysia, and Indonesia. Cambodia, however, opposed. It reasoned that the ruling was not accepted by all parties including China, a key ASEAN Dialogue Partner (Beech, 2016), and that ASEAN should be cautious in not exacerbating tensions on a complex matter.

An impasse seemed imminent. Laos, however, saw two ways to break the deadlock. First, the phrase, "full respect for legal and diplomatic processes", was proposed to be inserted under the section on ASEAN

Community Building, in a way that everyone could agree on. Second, Laos would issue a Chairman's Statement instead of a Joint Communique for the AMM if the first option failed to draw a consensus. Extensive efforts ensued in explaining to and lobbying concerned parties.

On the day of the AMM, Laos proposed the first option. Brunei, known as a "silent claimant state" for its non-confrontational approach on the issue, was the first to support it. It endorsed the proposal as a good way out for ASEAN and praised the Lao SOM leader's extensive experience in international negotiation and diplomacy, as well as in-depth knowledge of ASEAN. The Philippines, Cambodia, Vietnam and Malaysia also voiced their agreement, with the rest of the members (Singapore, Myanmar, Thailand, and Indonesia) congratulating Laos as the Chair. The Joint Communique was adopted.

Some critics may dismiss the language as watered down, but the consensus itself was a breakthrough. This is because inserting the phrase "full respect for legal and diplomatic processes" in the section on ASEAN community building would satisfy all sides. It was a way out for both the Philippines and Vietnam – which gave some acknowledgement of the ruling as it is a legal process – as well as Cambodia, since the communique did not explicitly mention the ruling or the legal process in the specific paragraph on the South China Sea.

Laos was widely lauded for its steady stewardship of ASEAN in 2016. The Economist stated: "Laos Chairmanship of ASEAN appears to have successfully rebalanced the country's … priorities towards a focus on relations with both China and ASEAN." The Nation newspaper of Thailand also gave Laos its due credit: "Kudos to ASEAN Chair

Laos despite hiccups" (Chongkittavorn, 2016). The Straits Times of Singapore said "the summits went smoothly… due to Laos' commendable stewardship, which surprised many ASEAN watchers" (Tang, 2016). Finally, as one diplomat told The Laotian Times: "There was a lot of wisdom in the way the Chair came up with the formula on this highly complex and sensitive issue" (Savankham, 2016).

That the 2016 ASEAN Summit was able to release statements without objection could be attributed to the perception held by all key players, including China and the US: Laos was neither a protégé nor enemy of anyone, and it had tried its best to secure outcomes palatable to all.

No Drama and Soft Power: Laos' International Cultural Engagements

The competence and image of a country can neither rely or be judged solely on its achievements or failures at the high table of ASEAN or world politics. Since the end of the Cold War and the start of its ASEAN membership, Laos has made and encouraged efforts by government and non-government entities to brand the country as a place of unique attraction that mixes tradition and modernity, and worthy of a visit, a stay and further discovery.

Tourism

The long-term political stability of Laos is one of its greatest assets, burnishing its reputation as a peaceful nation. This has made Laos a coveted destination for tourists, including those wishing to see a developing country undergoing rapid transition or catch a glimpse of Southeast Asia as it was in the past. Recently, while Laos has handled the situation relatively well, compared to other nations, the pandemic has decimated the tourism sector. A travel campaign titled *Lao Thiao Lao* (Lao Visit Laos) was launched to boost domestic tourism with a widely popular Facebook Page. It contains breathtaking images of the country and its plethora of tourism sites and local eateries captioned with both Lao and English text. In revealing aspects of Laos that have never been seen before, it could well be the foundation of a successful regional, if not global, marketing effort.

Entertainment

Laos' conservative traditional culture means it has typically shied away from sending women to compete in global beauty pageants. But this changed in 2017, when Laos decided to participate formally in international beauty competitions in an effort to showcase Lao culture and embrace modernity. Souphaphone Somvichit became the first Lao woman to compete in the Miss Universe pageant (Yap, 2017). In 2018, Laos' second Miss Universe contestant won Best National Costume (Savanhkham, 2018). While it did not win the crown, Laos' flair and creativity won hearts around the world, as the few minutes of airtime translated to much international media attention.

Laos is also known for hosting the Luang Prabang Film Festival, a film event that showcases Southeast Asia's top films to audiences beyond the region. Mention Laos' nascent film industry and the first name to pop up is often Mattie Do, the country's first female filmmaker. Her feature-length films have brought much attention to Laos – *Dearest Sister* was the country's first submission for Best Foreign Language Film at the 90th Academy Awards in 2017, while *The Long Walk* was selected as part of Giornate degli Autori at the Venice International Film Festival in 2019. Lao cultural elements were also incorporated into the latest

Disney hit *Raya and the Last Dragon*, with characters *Boun* and *Noi* – both typical Lao names – playing important roles.

Media

Laos maintains several state-run traditional news outlets that convey information related to government policies and current events to foreign readers. Among the most reputable is the English-language *Vientiane Times*, the print and online editions of which are widely read and consistently cited by international media. Another is *Khaosan Pathet Lao* (KPL), which offers online news in both English and French, while the *Lao National Television* (LNTV) offers regular news broadcasts on TV and social media in English. The digital-born *The Laotian Times* news portal has embraced Facebook as its go-to distribution channel, and is breaking new ground by countering the pervasive narrative of Laos as a tiny, reclusive, colonial backwater that is often pushed by international media. *Champa Meuanglao* magazine, the inflight publication of the national carrier Lao Airlines, furnishes memorable snapshots of the country's scenery, sites, and culture to first-time visitors and regional frequent flyers to Laos. Several other outlets, both digital and print, are maintained for non-English speaking audiences such as Chinese, Vietnamese, and Thai.

Cultural Exchanges

Music and dance have played an integral part in Laos' mission to engage with the world, particularly parts of the diaspora in the United States. One example is the cultural exchange programmes by the US and Lao governments and the Pom Foundation, whereby national artists from the Lao National School of Music and Dance are invited to engage with American audiences through traditional live music and dance performances. The Pom Foundation has also hosted two-week cultural youth camps in various cities, during which music and cultural arts professors shared knowledge of their craft with students. Similar exchange programmes have been organised between Laos and Japan, Korea, China, Vietnam, and Thailand.

Conclusion

For some, Laos is a small country sandwiched between bigger neighbours that is subjected to the external power plays of larger forces. For others, it is perceived as an undeveloped country known better as a nostalgic and exotic travel destination. For many, it does not even exist - either ignorant of its existence or geographical location, or worse, deem the country too unimportant to give it any thought. But Laos has come a long way.

Both the government and society are making conscious efforts to project a more balanced image of the country as independent, capable, and boasting unique charms. As its commendable stewardship of ASEAN and myriad cross-cultural efforts have shown, Laos has much to offer in both formal diplomacy and soft power.

Anoulak Kittikhoun

Anoulak Kittikhoun is the Chief Strategy and Partnership Officer of the Mekong River Commission (MRC), in charge of strategic planning and international cooperation. A graduate of the Australian National University and the City University of New York, his books include *River Basin Organizations in Water Diplomacy* and *Small Countries, Big Diplomacy: Laos in the UN, ASEAN and MRC.*

Aditta Kittikhoun

Aditta Kittikhoun is the Senior Partner of RDK Group, a Laos-based boutique media and marketing firm that specialises in communications and PR strategy. A graduate of the Macaulay Honors College at Hunter College of New York and Oxford University, he has been integral in marketing numerous national-level projects.

References

Beech, H, "What a Retracted Statement Says About China's Growing Power in the South China Sea," Time, 15 June 2016, https://time.com/4369660/asean-south-china-sea-statement/

Chongkittavorn, K., "Kudos to ASEAN Chair Laos Despite Hiccups," The Nation, 18 September 2016, https://www.nationthailand.com/opinion/30295635

Cultural Exchange. Pom Foundation. https://www.pomfoundation.org/culturalexchange.

Kittikhoun A. & Kittikhoun A., Small Countries, Big Diplomacy: Laos at the UN, ASEAN and MRC, New York and London: Routledge, 2021, in press.

Permanent Court of Arbitration, "PCA Press Release: The South China Sea Arbitration (The Republic of the Philippines v. The People's Republic of China)," 12 July 2016, https://pca-cpa.org/en/news/pca-press-release-the-south-china-sea-arbitration-the-republic-of-the-philippines-v-the-peoples-republic-of-china/

Pholsena, V., "LAOS IN 2004: Towards Subregional Integration: 10 Years On." Southeast Asian Affairs, 2005, pp. 179.

Savankham, F., "Why Laos' Chairmanship of ASEAN and Related Summits was a Success," The Laotian Times, 16 September 2016, https://laotiantimes.com/2016/09/16/why-laos-chairmanship-of-asean-and-related-summits-was-a-success

Savanhkham, F., "On-anong Captures National Costume Gong for Laos at Miss Universe 2018," 17 December 2018, https://laotiantimes.com/2018/12/17/laos-national-costume-gong-miss-universe-2018/

Tang, S.M., "Six Takeaways from the ASEAN Summits," The Straits Times, 15 September 2016, https://www.straitstimes.com/opinion/six-takeaways-from-asean-summits

Yap, J., "Meet History's First Miss Universe Laos," The Laotian Times, 27 August 2017, https://laotiantimes.com/2017/08/27/meet-historys-first-miss-universe-laos

Malaysia

"As a developing nation-state, Malaysia has become a middle power and a leader of the developing world, owing to its strength in promoting traditional and formal diplomacy. However, the world is changing rapidly with the emergence of disruptive technologies, geopolitical tensions and black swan events such as COVID-19. There is a pressing need for states to cooperate not only with other states but also with non-state actors within these states."

Petronas Towers, Kuala Lumpur

Rethinking Public Diplomacy in Malaysia

Michael O. K. Yeoh
Zaim Mohzani

If there is one thing the COVID-19 pandemic has clearly demonstrated, it is that no nation-state is able to address this global issue by itself. Instead, states have had to cooperate with other states as well as with non-state actors such as multinational corporations and civil society. In this context, public diplomacy plays an ever more critical role in building trust and cooperation between the public and states. While Malaysia has punched above its weight to become a middle power through formal diplomacy, its public diplomacy efforts can be enhanced.

This article suggests three growth areas in public diplomacy for Malaysia to explore: youth diplomacy, TechPlomacy and think tank diplomacy. Even as states remain the principal actors in international relations, the increasingly complex challenges of the 21st century will require states to embrace multistakeholderism, especially with foreign non-state actors. Ultimately, global challenges require global, not national, solutions.

To start off, what does "public diplomacy" actually mean? Simply put, it is the practice of a state in communicating with foreign publics to inform or influence their attitudes in supporting or tolerating its foreign policy (Hunt, 2016). It is not a new concept as public diplomacy long predates the term itself (Huijgh, 2016). Dr Nicholas Cull (2008), an expert in this field, states the components of public diplomacy as listening, advocacy, cultural diplomacy, exchange and international broadcasting. Closer to home, Jean Tan of the Singapore International Foundation (2018) presents a useful framework of public diplomacy as five dimensions with increasing engagement: awareness, appreciation, affinity, advocacy and action.

It is important to note that public diplomacy is not propaganda, as former diplomat Alan Hunt (2016) distinguishes the latter as "deliberate direction, or even manipulation, of information". It is also worth noting that the end goal of public diplomacy is closely related with the concept of "soft power", coined by Joseph Nye (1990). According to Nye (2008), soft power is "the ability to affect others to obtain the outcomes one wants through attraction rather than coercion or payment". Nye argues that soft power does not replace hard power (i.e. military and economic). Rather, states should combine hard and soft power or "smart power".

The concepts of public diplomacy and soft power are often used interchangeably by policy-makers; however, they are distinctively different. Public diplomacy should be understood as a state's tool in the context of its soft power (Nye, 2008). Just as soft power complements hard power, public diplomacy complements traditional or formal diplomacy.

The next question worth asking is: What are examples of public diplomacy? States have been investing heavily in public diplomacy with varying degrees of success. The United Kingdom (UK) makes for a worthy case study. The British Council's budget in 2019 was over US$1.7 billion and it has reached 791 million people in over 100 nations. The UK Foreign, Commonwealth and Development Office has spent close to US$157 million on the Chevening Scholarships from April 2018 to September 2020 alone. The scholarship has directly impacted over 50,000 recipients from over 160 nations, including Malaysia and Singapore. The British Broadcasting Corporation (BBC), heavily supported by the UK government, is arguably its most powerful public diplomacy tool, broadcasting to a global audience of 468.2 million across 42 languages in 2020.

The British public diplomacy is by no means an outlier. One only needs to look at the efforts of other states for the importance they place on public diplomacy — the United States (e.g. Fulbright Program, International Visitor Leadership Program), France (Alliance Française), Germany (Goethe-Institut) and China (Confucius Institute, China Central Television).

However, public diplomacy is not the exclusive domain of major or great powers. For example, when Switzerland's reputation was damaged by revelations that its banking system was complicit in handling Nazi gold during World War II, the Swiss government through its "Presence Switzerland" unit aggressively engaged key opinion leaders from 2000 to 2007 to successfully rebrand its image (Cull, 2008). Cull provides a useful qualification in understanding successful public diplomacy efforts: "Sound policy is the best public diplomacy in any case."

In the context of public diplomacy in Southeast Asia, this article concurs with Jean Tan's view that public diplomacy is not prominent in policy discourse in Singapore and the region, including Malaysia. Despite Malaysia's success as a middle power, its lack of emphasis on public diplomacy prevents it from promoting its values, culture and interests globally. Instead, Malaysia owes much of its success to its investment in Track 1 or formal diplomacy – between states.

Examples range from the first Prime Minister Tunku Abdul Rahman's peacekeeping operations in Congo and his successor Tun Abdul Razak Hussein's propagation of Zone of Peace, Freedom and Neutrality (ZOPFAN) and Non-Alignment Movement (NAM) to Tun Dr Mahathir Mohamad's legacy of closer cooperation with South-South, Asia-Pacific Economic Cooperation (APEC), and Organisation of Islamic Cooperation (OIC) nations (Ruhanie, 2019).

Malaysia's public diplomacy, however, paints a different picture. There are notable examples of Malaysia's public initiatives. Top of the list is the Malaysian Technical Cooperation Programme (MTCP), initiated in 1978, that has been instrumental in promoting South-South cooperation by sharing Malaysia's development experience with other states – particularly those in Africa – through technical cooperation programmes (MATRADE, 2021).

In addition, Malaysia Kitchen Programme (MKP) was introduced in 2006 to promote and brand Malaysia's cuisine throughout the world by providing financing facilities to Malaysian entrepreneurs and restaurateurs abroad (MITI, 2015). However, MKP has largely faded into obscurity. Interestingly, gastrodiplomacy is a recurring theme in

Malaysia's public diplomacy. For instance, the Agrobazaar Malaysia in Singapore was launched by Malaysia's sixth Prime Minister Dato' Sri Najib Razak and his counterpart, Mr Lee Hsien Loong, in 2014 to much fanfare (Tan, 2014). Designed to be a hub for Malaysian fruits for Singaporeans to enjoy, it eventually closed down.

Based on conversations with Malaysian Ministry of Foreign Affairs officials, the lack of continuity in many programmes could be attributed to various factors: financial constraints, shift in priorities with changing administrations and lack of strategic national framework for public diplomacy.

What could Malaysia do to rethink its public diplomacy? While this article acknowledges the various constraints on developing impactful and meaningful public diplomacy strategic initiatives, Malaysia should pick the low-hanging fruits. There are three growth areas Malaysia can explore to enhance its public diplomacy:

1. Youth Diplomacy
Close to half of Malaysia's – and ASEAN's – population are below 35 years (ASEAN, 2017). Beyond the formal channels, specifically the ASEAN Ministerial Meeting on Youth (AMMY), there is little engagement with the youth by the states. Thus, youth diplomacy remains a largely untapped area for Malaysia and ASEAN member states.

In fact, the US recognised this gap and initiated the successful Young Southeast Asian Leaders Initiative (YSEALI), which has directly engaged over 150,000 young leaders in the region (US Mission to ASEAN, 2020). Initiatives such as the Singapore International

Foundation's ASEAN Youth Fellowship should also be replicated by Malaysia in collaboration with the ASEAN Secretariat.

In fact, there is a mushrooming of youth-based civil society organisations (CSOs) and social enterprises with an ASEAN focus such as Malaysian Youth Diplomacy (MyDiplomacy), Indonesian Youth Diplomacy (IYD) and ASEAN Youth Organization. Malaysia should capitalise on its predominantly young population and sponsor initiatives such as exchange programmes, leadership fellowship and Model ASEAN to connect its youth with those from other ASEAN member states.

A more radical — but entirely feasible — idea is drawn from Malaysian Youth Parliament: establishing an "ASEAN Youth Assembly", where elected youth representatives from member states would deliberate on regional issues encompassing the three pillars of ASEAN (Zaim, 2016).

2. TechPlomacy (Technological Diplomacy)

In August 2017, Denmark became the first country to appoint a "Tech Ambassador" to major technology companies – Amazon, Google, Facebook, Baidu, Alibaba, Tencent – based in the US and China. Recognising the "diplomatic deficit" of traditional diplomacy (confined to states) and disruptive impact of emerging technologies on international relations, the Tech Ambassador is mandated to engage Big Tech to influence the direction of technology development as well as the global agenda on key technology questions through multi-stakeholder partnerships (Office of Denmark's Tech Ambassador, 2021).

Ever since the inception of TechPlomacy, states such as Germany, France, Estonia, Slovakia and Australia have appointed a Digital or

Cyber Ambassador (Klynge et al., 2020). While Malaysia may seem far removed from tech policy discussions in Silicon Valley and Beijing, Big Tech's impact is pervasive and impacts all Malaysian and ASEAN citizens. Malaysia need not appoint its own Tech Ambassador, but it can leverage its global diaspora, especially in the US, and appoint a prominent Malaysian business leader of a US-based tech company to be an "Honorary Tech Consul" of Malaysia to Silicon Valley.

Malaysia should also play a more proactive role in raising technology issues at the ASEAN level. For example, Malaysia can initiate dialogue with technologists, CSOs and entrepreneurs on initiating an "ASEAN Artificial Intelligence (AI) Strategy" to not only develop AI capabilities among member states but also define the ethics and governance framework pertaining to AI use.

3. Think Tank Diplomacy

Despite the prominent role think tanks play in facilitating Track 2 (informal) diplomacy, their role in Malaysian public diplomacy still remains largely unexploited. Regional forums such as the annual Shangri-La Dialogue and Asia-Pacific Roundtable have provided an avenue for non-state actors to engage in dialogue with states on key issues such as the South China Sea dispute. These Track 2 diplomacy events can deepen bilateral and multilateral relations.

Going further, Malaysia could sponsor and support a network or coalition of think tanks in Kuala Lumpur to bridge the divide between the East and the West, especially in the context of the US-China strategic competition. As Kishore Mahbubani (2008) and Parag Khanna (2019) rightfully argue, the balance of power will shift from the Western world to Asia and consequently, this rivalry will likely become more intense. Malaysia, with its diverse population, can be the ideal host for high-level summits for think tanks to build trust and confidence between states in both hemispheres.

According to the Global Go To Think Tank Index (McGann, 2020), there are close to 2,000 think tanks in Asia alone. In complementing Malaysia's traditional diplomacy, think tank diplomacy can promote closer relations with its key partners in the 3As – ASEAN, APEC and Arab (Middle Eastern) nations (Yeoh, 2019). Think tank diplomacy should be fully explored and exploited to build bridges.

As a developing nation-state, Malaysia has become a middle power and a leader of the developing world, owing to its strength in promoting traditional and formal diplomacy. However, the world is changing rapidly with the emergence of disruptive technologies, geopolitical tensions and black swan events such as COVID-19. There is a pressing need for states to cooperate not only with other states but also with non-state actors within these states.

To achieve that, public diplomacy is an important tool for states to communicate their strategic priorities and values with foreign publics. Initiatives, exemplified by the UK's BBC, US' YSEALI and France's Alliance Française, have demonstrated its effectiveness. Despite Malaysia's attempts such as MTCP, Global Movement of Moderates (GMM) and MKP, they are still largely inadequate.

Although encumbered by financial, political and administrative constraints, Malaysia should explore these three low-hanging fruits in public diplomacy. Through youth diplomacy, Malaysia can tap its young population to build confidence and cooperation with fellow ASEAN states by engaging their respective youth communities. TechPlomacy allows Malaysia to engage its global diaspora to communicate its interests to Big Tech while working with entrepreneurs and technologists in ASEAN to shape regional frameworks on emerging technologies.

Malaysia can also be the ideal bridge between the East and the West in reconnecting and rebuilding trust through think tank diplomacy. Malaysia is well-poised and well-positioned to exploit these – and many more – forms of public diplomacy in its journey to become an even more impactful middle and regional power.

Michael Yeoh

Michael Yeoh is the President of KSI Strategic Institute for Asia Pacific, a Kuala Lumpur-based think tank. He is a public intellectual, thought leader and social entrepreneur. He was a co-founder of the Asian Strategy and Leadership Institute.

Zaim Mohzani

Zaim Mohzani is the Director of Government, Diplomatic and Youth Engagement at the KSI Strategic Institute for Asia Pacific. A passionate community builder, he has founded three award-winning non-governmental organisations that have impacted 10,000 young Malaysians.

References

Association of Southeast Asian Nations (ASEAN). *First ASEAN Youth Development Index*, July 2017, ASEAN, https://asean.org/storage/2017/10/ASEAN-UNFPA_report_web-final-05sep.pdf

BBC Media Centre. "Tony Hall: UK must "unleash the full global potential of the BBC" - as new all time record global audience is announced." 23 July 2020, https://www.bbc.co.uk/mediacentre/latestnews/2020/global-reach

British Council. *Annual Report and Accounts 2018-19*, https://www.britishcouncil.org/sites/default/files/2018-2019-annual-report-final.pdf

Cull, Nicholas J. "Public Diplomacy: Taxonomies and Histories." *The Annals of the American Academy of Political and Social Science*, vol. 616, no. 1, 2008, pp. 31-54.

Huijgh, Ellen. "Public Diplomacy." *The SAGE Handbook of Diplomacy*, (eds.) Costas M. Constantinou, Pauline Kerr, and Paul Sharp, SAGE Publications, 2016, pp. 437-450.

Hunt, Alan. "Definitions of Public Diplomacy." *Public Diplomacy*, United Nations Institute for Training and Research (UNITAR), New York, 2016, pp. 17-24.

Gilboa, Eytan. "Digital Diplomacy." *The SAGE Handbook of Diplomacy*, (eds.) Costas M. Constantinou, Pauline Kerr, and Paul Sharp, SAGE Publications, 2016, pp. 540-551.

Khanna, Parag. *The Future Is Asian: Global Order In The Twenty-First Century*, Weidenfeld & Nicolson: London, 2019.

Klynge, Casper, Mikael Ekman and Nikolaj Juncher Waedegaard. "Diplomacy in the Digital Age: Lessons from Denmark's TechPlomacy Initiative." *The Hague Journal of Diplomacy*, vol. 15, no. 1-2, 2020, pp. 1-11.

Mahbubani, Kishore. *Has the West Lost It? A Provocation*, New Delhi: Allen Lane, 2018.

MATRADE. "Malaysian Technical Cooperation Programme (MTCP)." *MATRADE's Success Stories*, 2021, https://www.matrade.gov.my/en/about-matrade/achievements/matrade-success-stories/malaysian-technical-cooperation-programme-mtcp

McGann, James G. "2019 Global Go To Think Tank Index Report." TTCSP Global Go To Think Tank Index Reports, no. 17. 2020, https://repository.upenn.edu/cgi/viewcontent.cgi?article=1018&context=think_tanks

Ministry of International Trade and Industry (MITI). "Malaysian Kitchen Programme (MKP)." *MITI Blog*, 22 June 2015, https://www.miti.gov.my/index.php/blogs/view/295.

Nye Jr., Joseph S. *Bound to Lead: The Changing Nature of American Power*, New York: Simon and Schuster, 1990.

Nye Jr., Joseph S. "Public Diplomacy and Soft Power." *The ANNALS of the American Academy of Political and Social Science*, vol. 616, no. 1, March 2008, pp. 94-109.

Office of Denmark's Tech Ambassador. "TechPlomacy (technological-diplomacy)." *Ministry of Foreign Affairs of Denmark*, 2021, https://techamb.um.dk/techplomacy

Ruhanie Ahmad. "Malaysia, a middle power?" *New Straits Times*, 12 March 2019, https://www.nst.com.my/opinion/columnists/2019/03/468227/malaysia-middle-power

Tan, Ben. "Agro-bazaar Promotes Malaysian Products, Launch Pad to Access New International Markets: Najib." *New Straits Times*, 27 August 2014, https://www.nst.com.my/news/2015/09/agro-bazaar-promotes-malaysian-products-launch-pad-access-new-international-markets

Tan, Jean. "The Rise of the Citizen Diplomat." *Singapore Magazine*, no. 2, 2018, Singapore International Foundation, pp.14-17, https://singaporemagazine.sif.org.sg/-/media/Project/Singapore-International-Foundation/Singapore-Magazine/e-Magazine/2018/SINGAPORE-Magazine-2018-Issue-2.pdf

U.S. Mission to ASEAN. "United States and ASEAN: A Billion Futures Across the Indo-Pacific." Office of the Spokesperson, 13 November 2020, https://asean.usmission.gov/united-states-and-asean-a-billion-futures-across-the-indo-pacific/

United Kingdom Government. *ODA Programme Spend by the FCO - Arms Length Bodies and Soft Power Programme Spend and Background information*, updated 10 December 2020, https://www.gov.uk/government/publications/official-development-assistance-oda-arms-length-bodies-and-soft-power-programmes

Yeoh, Michael Oon Kheng. "Punching our weight in international relations." *The Star*, 25 September 2019, https://www.thestar.com.my/opinion/letters/2019/09/25/punching-our-weight-in-international-relations

Zaim Mohzani. "Southeast Asia's Youth: The Need to Engage." *Focus*, no. 2, 2015, Institute of Strategic & International Studies (ISIS) Malaysia, https://isis.org.my/wp-content/uploads/2016/05/images_files_2016_isisfocus_isis_focus_issue-2-2016.pdf, pp. 16-17.

Myanmar

"*Though once actively holding soft power ambitions, Myanmar in recent decades has largely pursued a more defensive brand of public diplomacy, mainly seeking to justify legitimacy and performance at home and abroad.*"

Shwedagon Pagoda, Yangon

Myanmar's Public Diplomacy Experience and Challenges: Can ASEAN Make a Difference?

Moe Thuzar

G overnments around the globe employ some form of public diplomacy as a strategy to boost their country's, and by extension the ruling party's, image and credibility as competent and capable participants in international cooperation and collaboration. National interest, particularly the interest to survive and thrive in a competitive global environment, lies at the core of even the most innocuous and unassuming of public diplomacy efforts.

The nature of public diplomacy, which seeks to communicate, inform and persuade through various forms of interaction and exchanges, has opened up new horizons for nations and governments to share and discuss ideas, views and perspectives, and thus find a common understanding beyond conventional notions of "my country, right or wrong". Indeed, the two-way exchange of ideas through interactions facilitated by public diplomacy in today's interdependent world offers governments and peoples a more constructive principle that American

Senator Carl Schurz emphasised in 1871: "My country, right or wrong; if right, to be kept right; and if wrong, to be set right."

In this essay, I reflect on how Southeast Asia in the 21st century has adopted this kinder, gentler, less "in-your-face" approach to public diplomacy, with the Association of Southeast Asian Nations (ASEAN) community-building project forming an extension of, and a platform for, individual and collective public diplomacy approaches by the various Southeast Asian nations.

Against this Southeast Asian or ASEAN backdrop, I discuss the public diplomacy experiences and challenges of Myanmar (formerly Burma) over the past decades. Though once actively holding soft power ambitions, Myanmar in recent decades has largely pursued a more defensive brand of public diplomacy, mainly seeking to justify legitimacy and performance at home and abroad.

Public Diplomacy in Southeast Asia: From Nation Branding to People's Diplomacy

In the post-World War II and Cold War years, Southeast Asian nations were in various stages of emerging from colonial rule and/or the ravages of war. Nation-building was "an immediate and pressing task" (Wang, 2005). To this end, public diplomacy initiatives inevitably focused on seeking development assistance and technical cooperation. Senior government leaders were closely involved in the formulation and implementation of such initiatives. Personal diplomacy became a part of Southeast Asia's public diplomacy moves; national leaders led efforts to present investor-friendly, politically stable images of their nations, replete with economic potential and a capable workforce. (Wang, 2005).

Regional cooperation initiatives emerged out of such efforts too, so as to better navigate and balance geopolitical uncertainties and tensions of the times. The Non-Aligned Movement was born from the Asia-Africa Conference in Bandung, Indonesia, in 1955 to present a collective voice amidst rising Cold War tensions. ASEAN was established in 1967 to stave off the spread of communism in the region. Burma in the 1950s was one of the key convenors of the Bandung Conference, but Burma under socialist rule in 1967 declined to be a founding member of ASEAN.

ASEAN member states view regional cooperation and collaboration as important mechanisms that advance the policy interests and international image of the individual member states. They also see the grouping as a representative whole for Southeast Asia as a region. The regional element certainly gives more effect to individual and collective soft power projection, as regional collaboration emphasises the importance of partnerships and networks, a rules-based environment and promoting competitive advantages of talent and location as attractions. These are all important parts of the public diplomacy toolkit.

ASEAN's soft power success was such that its "demonstration effect" of developing through bilateral, regional and international cooperation drew the interest of closed economies such as Vietnam, Cambodia, Laos and Myanmar to be part of the ASEAN project. Indeed, the interest to be an ASEAN member led Myanmar to identify itself clearly as part of Southeast Asia.

Certain Southeast Asian nations, however, retain more salience in global perceptions. Indonesia, for instance, is often viewed as a success story of public diplomacy efforts to turn around negative perceptions after the

1997 Asian financial crisis and the views towards Islam in the post-9/11 environment. Yet, Singapore is the only Southeast Asian nation on the University of Southern California's Center on Public Diplomacy's Soft Power 30 index. In 2019, it ranked 21st out of the 30 countries on the list.

Another report, the Lowy Institute's annual Asia Power Index in 2020, showed ASEAN members Singapore, Thailand and Malaysia in the top 10 out of the 26 countries surveyed. Indonesia and Vietnam followed closely behind at 11th and 12th respectively, and the Index highlighted Vietnam as reaping the "greatest gains" compared to previous years. Myanmar, under the National League for Democracy (NLD) government, ranked 20th, after Brunei and ahead of Cambodia and Laos.

A closer look at the two reports and their themes highlight the trends that inform and influence the re-emergence of public diplomacy in the 21st century as an important element of foreign policy. The Soft Power Index lists six sub-indices: enterprise, digital, culture, education, engagement and government. Singapore ranked 1st for enterprise but scored low on engagement and culture. The Asia Power Index uses eight thematic measures of (hard and soft) power, including diplomatic and cultural influence, as well as economic capability and resilience.

The ASEAN community-building project, which continues as a work in progress for regional integration, places emphasis on governments working together, and increasingly with non-state actors (via Track 2 policy conversations among think tanks in ASEAN, or by engaging civil society and youth at the annual ASEAN Summits). Each ASEAN member state now links domestic development goals to ASEAN's regional development goals. Individual public diplomacy initiatives are also linked to the regional effort to promote the region's collective capacity and competence to external partners and investors. Yet, ASEAN's soft power does not seem as salient to Southeast Asians. The 2021 State of Southeast Asia survey conducted by the ISEAS-Yusof Ishak Institute's ASEAN Studies Centre showed that Southeast Asians prefer Japan for tourism, and the United States (US) for tertiary education. However, were choices for tourism limited to the region, Thailand, Singapore and Vietnam rank the highest.

Still, Vietnam's gains in economic and diplomatic reach after it joined ASEAN in 1995, and Myanmar's motives for wide-ranging political, administrative and economic reforms in 2011 (economic reform goals were formulated to be consistent with the ASEAN Economic Community goals), point to ASEAN's soft power success. The military coup in Myanmar on 1 February 2021, however, has placed ASEAN's image and credibility on the line as well as set back any incremental gains for Myanmar in the public diplomacy realm.

Myanmar's Public Diplomacy Experience and Challenges
During Burma's post-independence heyday, when it had parliamentary democracy in the 1950s, a morality play became an important instrument for the country's foreign and domestic policy moves. Burma's first post-independence Prime Minister U Nu authored a play to caution the Burmese public against domestic insurgencies of which communists were one of many factions taking up arms against the government.

Despite efforts by Nu to separate the domestic and international contexts of communism, the play came to be interpreted as Burma's stand against international communist aggression. To date, it stands as the only Burmese play to have been adapted into a feature-length film by Hollywood, via the "good offices" of the US Embassy in Rangoon. Yet, all Nu had wanted was to uphold his neutralist credentials in the Cold War world, and offer his services (never taken up) to negotiate some understanding between the US and China.

Despite a place in history as the co-founder of the Non-Aligned Movement, Burma's foreign policy projection did not find further voice after a military coup in 1962, which saw Nu's Defence Minister and Commander-in-Chief General Ne Win entrench his position as the country's leader for the next quarter-century. Ne Win continued Nu's foreign policy, but nuanced it as an "independent" foreign policy in 1971, and added an "active" element to that policy a decade later. Ne Win was active in his personal diplomacy efforts, too, especially with the leaders of the founding ASEAN member states, despite having declined to join the grouping in 1967.

While external powers pragmatically accepted Ne Win's taking over of state power in Burma in the context of Cold War era geopolitical considerations, attitudes were different towards the State Law and Order Restoration Council (SLORC, later renamed State Peace and Development Council or SPDC) that held power between 1988 and 2011. Isolated as a pariah state, the SLORC/SPDC turned to public diplomacy to seek a legitimacy that it never successfully gained.

In 1993, a SLORC "special diplomatic mission" did a two-month tour of the United Kingdom, Austria, Germany, the US, Australia, Hong Kong and Japan to explain "objective conditions and developments in Myanmar", meeting with former US President Jimmy Carter, then Australian Foreign Minister Gareth Evans and Japanese parliamentarians, and giving talks to invited audiences via think tank platforms. This was the first instance of a conscious effort at public diplomacy by the military regime, followed by Myanmar's participation at several ASEAN forums organised by think tanks in the network of the ASEAN Institutes of Strategic and International Studies (ASEAN-ISIS).

The Myanmar Institute of Strategic and International Studies (MISIS), established in 1992, organised several workshops with a similar intent to "explain the situation in Myanmar" throughout the SPDC years, to regional and international interlocutors. An observer at the ASEAN-ISIS table, MISIS became a full member in the network only during the Union Solidarity Development Party (USDP) government led by President Thein Sein. Myanmar's public diplomacy moves saw an uptick in the USDP years, with MISIS as the key actor engaging with other think tanks in the Track 2 policy discussions.

The largest gathering to date in 2014 of civil society organisations in Myanmar – for the ASEAN Civil Society Conference during Myanmar's ASEAN Chairmanship year – brought some hope for a wider role for non-state actors in public diplomacy. But the NLD government focused instead on a people-centred diplomacy, nuancing this approach in 2016 as one that would engage with neighbours and external partners on human security issues such as labour migration, and promoting more people-to-people contacts and exchanges.

Sadly, at the time of writing, the military coup of 1 February 2021 has disrupted Myanmar's democratic transition, and the nascent potential for further gains in soft power projection over the past decade. International criticism of the State Administration Council (SAC) military regime in Myanmar, and scepticism that the SAC would uphold the promises it made for stabilising the economy and re-establishing democracy in the country, will make any public diplomacy initiative by the SAC an uphill task, even as SAC representatives participate in various ASEAN meetings and forums. Countering the devastating impact of the coup presents a challenge for Myanmar's public diplomacy efforts to continue along a trajectory similar to that of other ASEAN members in the foreseeable future.

Moe Thuzar

Moe Thuzar is a Fellow at the ISEAS-Yusof Ishak Institute, and Co-coordinator of the ISEAS Myanmar Studies Programme. She was previously lead researcher (socio-cultural) in the ASEAN Studies Centre at ISEAS.

References

Britannica, T. Editors of Encyclopaedia. "Public diplomacy." *Encyclopedia Britannica*, 11 July 2017, (https://www.britannica.com/topic/public-diplomacy, accessed 30 June 2021).

Burma Press Summary Volume VII, No. 8, August 1993 (https://www.burmalibrary.org/en/burma-press-summary-volume-vii-no-8-august-1993, accessed 2 July 2021).

Khurana, Simran. "The History of "My Country, Right or Wrong!" *ThoughtCo*, 23 March 2018 (https://www.thoughtco.com/my-country-right-or-wrong-2831839, accessed 2 July 2021).

Lowy Institute. *Asia Power Index*, Sydney: Lowy Institute, 2020 (https://power.lowyinstitute.org/downloads/lowy-institute-2020-asia-power-index-key-findings-report.pdf, accessed 3 July 2021).

Meyskens, Covell. "There Never Was a Cold War China", *Wilson Center*, 9 September 2020 (https://www.wilsoncenter.org/blog-post/there-never-was-cold-war-china, accessed 3 July 2021).

Ratih Indraswari Ma. "Cultural Diplomacy in ASEAN: Collaborative Efforts", *International Journal of Social Science and Humanity*, Vol. 5, No. 4, April 2015 (http://www.ijssh.org/papers/487-V10010.pdf, accessed 3 July 2021).

Seah, S. et al. *The State of Southeast Asia: 2021*, Singapore: ISEAS-Yusof Ishak Institute, 2021

Smith, Daniel J. "Public Diplomacy and the "Self" in Regional Organization: A Network Approach to Identity Formation, Image Formation, and ASEAN Community Building", *Exchange: The Journal of Public Diplomacy*, Vol. 5 [2014], Iss. 1, Art. 8, 2014 (https://surface.syr.edu/cgi/viewcontent.cgi?article=1046, accessed 3 July 2021).

Snow, Nancy. "Public Diplomacy and Propaganda: Rethinking Diplomacy in the Age of Persuasion", *E-International Relations*, 4 December 2012 (https://www.e-ir.info/2012/12/04/public-diplomacy-and-propaganda-rethinking-diplomacy-in-the-age-of-persuasion/, accessed 2 July 2021).

Somasundram, Premarani. "Public Diplomacy: An Emerging New Normal in Foreign Policy", *Ethos*, Issue 11, Civil Service College, Singapore, 14 August 2012 (https://www.csc.gov.sg/articles/public-diplomacy-an-emerging-new-normal-in-foreign-policy, accessed 30 June 2021).

Sukma, Rizal. "Soft Power and Public Diplomacy: The Case of Indonesia. In: Lee S.J., Melissen J. (eds) *Public Diplomacy and Soft Power in East Asia*. Palgrave Macmillan Series in Global Public Diplomacy. Palgrave Macmillan, New York. https://doi.org/10.1057/9780230118447_6

Teslik, Lee Hudson. "Nation Branding Explained", *Council on Foreign Relations*, 9 November 2007 (https://www.cfr.org/backgrounder/nation-branding-explained, accessed 2 July 2021).

USC Center on Public Diplomacy. "Public Diplomacy in Southeast Asia", 11 February 2021 (https://uscpublicdiplomacy.org/story/public-diplomacy-southeast-asia, accessed 3 July 2021).

USC Center on Public Diplomacy. "The Soft Power 30: A Global Ranking of Soft Power, 2019", Portland, 2019 (https://softpower30.com/wp-content/uploads/2019/10/The-Soft-Power-30-Report-2019-1.pdf, accessed 3 July 2021).

Wang, Gungwu. *Nation Building: Five Southeast Asian Histories*, edited by Gungwu Wang, Institute of Southeast Asian Studies, Singapore.

Philippines

"Public diplomacy is nation branding, but it is also responding to domestic pressures, or influencing partner countries. What public diplomacy should not be is propaganda, at least not alone."

Rizal Monument, Manila

Public Diplomacy in the Age of Digital Media

Julio S. Amador III

Public diplomacy in the Philippines is primarily the work of the Department of Foreign Affairs (DFA), evolving from providing public information services to one that is integral to the whole machinery of foreign affairs and diplomacy. It now involves managing domestic public concerns, sending signals to foreign governments, and including non-government tracks in policy discussions. Each is replete with issues that need to be handled carefully.

Domestic public concerns, for instance, primarily revolve around issues involving overseas Filipino workers, the South China Sea, and Philippine relations with the United States and China. This essay examines the evolution of public diplomacy, drawing primarily from the original work that was published by the DFA. Recent developments merit a review of the assumptions made in the publication including, among others, developments in the DFA's use of social media. The essay will conclude with some insights on the practice of public diplomacy in the Philippines.

In 2016, when the DFA published the groundbreaking *Handbook on Philippine Public Diplomacy* – a compilation of essays from public diplomacy practitioners, stakeholders and scholars in the field – the main focus areas were media relations, crisis communications, relationship with overseas Filipino communities, nation branding, Track 2 or informal diplomacy, and public diplomacy in the age of social media.

These were and are critical precisely because the DFA not only has to address international audiences, but also has to be more attentive to the domestic pulse. As essay contributors to the handbook Ambassador J. Eduardo Malaya and foreign service officer Sharon Agduma noted, fostering public understanding and support for the policies that DFA must implement "requires a level of openness and transparency which diplomats are often not used to".

One notable change, however, since the publication of the handbook is that the DFA currently does not have a spokesperson, as the Secretary of Foreign Affairs, Mr Teodoro L. Locsin Jr., popularly known as Teddyboy, acts as the de facto spokesperson given his ubiquitous Twitter presence. From announcements regarding the Philippine-US alliance to visas for foreign spouses of Filipinos, Locsin has announced, pronounced and walked back foreign policy. He has also used his online presence to improve assistance to Filipinos in the country and abroad by referring them to the DFA, or the appropriate Philippine embassy or consulate through Twitter.

The DFA's social media accounts, particularly Twitter and Facebook, are also actively used to disseminate information on consular developments or foreign policy statements. On Facebook, the DFA has been active in disseminating infographics regarding its COVID-19 activities such as the repatriation of Filipinos overseas, the Quincentennial Commemoration of the arrival of the Spaniards in the Philippines, public advisories and commemoration of the anniversaries of Philippine bilateral relations with other states.

On Twitter, the DFA replicates its Facebook posts but regularly tags Secretary Locsin so that he can retweet as needed. The DFA Twitter account also regularly responds to queries that Locsin sends its way. In particular, the DFA Twitter account had to answer questions related to COVID-19 including issues of passports, visas, entry of foreign nationals who are engaged or wed to Filipinos, citizens who needed to exit the Philippines for jobs abroad, migrants who got stuck in the country and sundry enquiries made online.

Philippine Embassies are also active particularly on Facebook, with official pages to relay embassy-specific concerns. Foreign service officers, particularly those designated with consular functions, are expected to respond to consular and other concerns through social media. Some of them created Facebook accounts that are titled after their consular functions to separate these from their personal ones. For some embassies, their Facebook pages are a good way to introduce the Philippines to their host countries, remind Filipinos overseas about their home country, and allow the embassy officials – particularly the ambassador – to show their respect to their host.

Apart from the DFA and its online presence, President Rodrigo Duterte's occasional national security and foreign affairs outbursts, which are usually newsworthy, also merit a discussion as public diplomacy must take into account the various crises created by these statements. President Duterte, for instance, publicly excoriated the United States' colonial atrocities in the Philippines in response to criticisms from a US legislator.

A positive effect of President Duterte's histrionics on history was the fast-tracking of the return of the Balangiga Bells, which were taken as spoils of war during the US pacification campaigns in the Philippines. He then upped the ante by ordering the termination of the visiting forces agreement between the Philippines and the US, a move which would impact the latter's ability to work with its ally particularly on humanitarian assistance and military training and exercises.

The presidential spokesperson also impacts public diplomacy, as he or she sometimes speaks on foreign policy issues to present the president's views. These views are on the same level as those of the foreign secretary, given that the spokesperson has ministerial rank and speaks for the president. President Duterte's spokespersons have all made statements on foreign policy and foreign affairs, which technically should have been left to the foreign ministry. But given the centralising nature of the presidency, their remarks would still be legitimately considered as the president's foreign policy statements.

Social Media Public Diplomacy

Social media has become a potent tool for the DFA to conduct its public diplomacy both for domestic and foreign audiences. Domestically, social media has become a tool for accountability and feedback to the DFA. Concerns about staff behaviour, passport issues and/or comments on foreign policy is evident on the DFA's social media accounts.

For its external audience, social media has also become an easier way to relay messages through statements both written and in video format. Foreign diplomats may find it easier to follow the Secretary of Foreign Affairs' tweets and get glimpses of the country's positions on certain issues than to secure appointments for meetings.

With social media, the days of the foreign ministry as the sole voice on foreign affairs – and the other ministries as speaking only to a domestic audience – are gone. The online platforms have ensured that there is no more divide between a domestic and an international audience. When the foreign secretary speaks or tweets to an international audience, Filipinos within the country can listen to or read these. When the presidential spokesperson or defense secretary speaks to an audience on domestic matters, social media guarantees that the remarks will be carried internationally.

Public diplomacy, therefore, has become both a domestic and international concern. To quote former DFA spokesperson Ambassador Malaya, the "challenge to the DFA public affairs office and public diplomacy practitioners, generally, is how to effectively communicate and make their cases before the various publics in a complex and democratised communications environment".

In many ways, the *Handbook on Philippine Public Diplomacy* has proven to be prescient. During the time of publication, the DFA and its stakeholders discussed public diplomacy in terms of crafting the diplomatic narrative, managing media relations, crisis communications, communicating with the diaspora, nation branding, the role of social media and Track 2 diplomacy. As one of the diplomats who wrote in the handbook noted, "public diplomacy is essentially a tool for achieving political ends". Public diplomacy is nation branding, but it is also responding to domestic pressures, or influencing partner countries. What public diplomacy should not be is propaganda, at least not alone.

As sources of information and intelligence become more open or have shifted to digital platforms, diplomats at post or decision-makers at home will have to find new ways of influencing friends and countering opponents. Foreign policy decision-makers will be able to create their own networks that at times will bypass their embassies. Hostile countries will also seek new ways to use public diplomacy as a tool to influence bilateral relations.

How can embassies or consulates influence views on their home countries when sources of information are abundant online? When expertise is readily available in online videos or various op-eds or research published online, how can diplomats make their own analyses and observations relevant to foreign policy decision-making? These are just some of the questions that the practice of diplomacy has to contend with in the Philippines and beyond.

Julio S. Amador III

Julio S. Amador III is Interim President at the Foundation for the National Interest. He was Director of the Performance and Projects Management Office-Security, Justice, and Peace Cluster at the Office of the Cabinet Secretary, Office of the President of the Philippines, from December 2017-November 2018.

Thailand

"*In the 2020s, public diplomacy will be more critical than ever to foreign policy as countries, particularly the small and medium nations in Southeast Asia, have witnessed intensifying geopolitical competition among the major powers.*"

Wwat Suthat and Sao Chingcha, Bangkok

The Evolution of Thai-Style Public Diplomacy

Seksan Anantasirikiat

Public diplomacy has gained a great deal of attention from both academia and practitioners these days as a foreign policy tool to inform and influence foreign publics. However, a plethora of scholarship focuses on the European and American regions. This article, therefore, narrows the gap in literature by analysing Thailand's public diplomacy.

It argues that the purpose of Thai public diplomacy is to project national image and create better understanding rather than to influence foreign publics. It also contends that international and domestic surroundings play an essential role in determining the purpose of public diplomacy.

Instead of exploring the case through the lens of Western scholars, the practice of Thai public diplomacy is conceptualised by tracing the government's actions back to the context of the Cold War and post-Cold War period. The final section looks at the future of Thai public diplomacy.

Waging the Information War in Southeast Asia

Thailand was agile not only in engaging with foreign publics and Thai nationals to project national presence in the international arena, but also in waging an information war against the communist ideology during the Cold War. The two main messengers at that time were the monarchy and the Ministry of Foreign Affairs.

The late King Bhumibol Adulyadej the Great, as the Head of State, zealously exercised his duty by visiting diverse countries, including Indonesia, France, Japan, New Zealand, Vietnam and the United States from 1959 to 1967. According to Supamit (2017), the King's visits were meaningful to his leading role in the country. He also engaged foreign publics on several occasions during his visits because he discerned their importance in the conduct of national diplomacy.

In 1965, the same year Edmund A. Gullion coined the term "public diplomacy", the Thai government established the Radio Free Asia (RFA) with the United States. The main station was located in Ayutthaya Province, a former capital city of Thailand. Three years later, RFA aired its first programme through the channel AM1575, under the supervision of the Broadcasting Division, part of the Department of Information at the Ministry of Foreign Affairs. The target group of this operation was Thai nationals living in Thailand and abroad.

In 1984, the Thai government inked an agreement with the United States to establish another radio station, aiming to broadcast the programmes from RFA and Voice of America (VOA) to other countries in the region. RFA's role had altered to (1) improve understanding between Thailand and its neighbours; and (2) inform Thai nationals of the duties and missions of the Ministry.

Winning Hearts and Minds the Thai Way

The practice of public diplomacy in Thailand had flourished after major shifts in global and regional situations. The country's foreign policy in the late 1980s became more outward-looking. One of the most well-known policies then was "Turning Indochina from a Battleground into a Marketplace" under General Chatichai Choonhavan's government. The objective of this policy was multi-dimensional: to attract foreign direct investment and advance regional economic cooperation.

In 1992, the Ministry annexed the practice of cultural diplomacy as a part of the country's public diplomacy by adopting the Basic Plan on Promoting International Cultural Relations. The plan categorised three groups of countries and indicated how to utilise cultural diplomacy to promote mutual understanding.

The first group covers Thailand's neighbouring countries, which are the most strategically important. Cultural diplomacy could bridge perception gaps and create a sense of community. The second group includes global and regional economic powers such as Australia, China, European countries, Japan, South Korea and the United States. Thailand could promote its cultural attractions to these countries in order to gain more confidence. The third group comprises countries in Africa, Latin America and South Asia, which could be potential markets in the future (Chantana, 2001). An example of this cultural diplomacy is the Thai Festival, which is held in other countries to showcase Thailand's cultural performances as well as its products and services.

However, the Asian Financial Crisis in 1997 halted the buildup of Thai public diplomacy. Instead, the country immediately embraced King Bhumibol's Sufficiency Economy Philosophy (SEP) as a parallel towards national development. Following the King's guidance, Thailand International Cooperation Agency (TICA) adapted the SEP for implementing the Sustainable Development Goals (SDGs) by underlining the importance of partnership (SDG 17) in international development. TICA has been actively promoting "SEP for SDGs" since 2003. One year later, the country re-oriented its status from aid recipient to development partner.

Apart from the Ministry, the monarchy has also played a constructive role in advocating development cooperation as part of Thai public diplomacy. There are six Royal Development Study Centers nationwide. These centres provide information and guidance on how to implement SEP for SDGs in real life. They are "study centres", where the representatives of developing countries can visit and learn. They also serve as field trip venues for international guests when they visit Thailand.

Princess Maha Chakri Sirindhorn, the daughter of the late King Bhumibol, has also initiated several royal projects aimed at narrowing the development gap in neighbouring and developing countries. These projects include agricultural development programmes in Laos, educational development programmes for primary and secondary schools in Myanmar, and vocational schools in Cambodia. The programmes denote Thailand's practice of caring and sharing towards its neighbours. They also reflect the key characteristics of the country as "Kingdom", where the monarchy has been responsible for improving people's well-being, and of "moderateness", a hallmark of the Thais.

More recently, Thailand has been among the countries lauded for keeping the COVID-19 pandemic under control due to various factors such as its high quality public health system; the social cohesion shown by the so-called "Happy Sharing Cabinet", a voluntary sharing of consumption goods by Thai people; and the contact tracing system in local areas. The Global COVID-19 Index (GCI) also noted that Thailand has the highest ability for recovery (PR Thai Government, 2020). The country's performance in dealing with difficult situations can be another feather in its public diplomacy cap, as it projects a positive national image and demonstrates its credibility to the world.

Working with Strategic Stakeholders

The Public Diplomacy Information Division, under the Department of Information at the Ministry of Foreign Affairs, has been responsible for the country's public diplomacy policy. Its mission also relates to the proactive dissemination of information to Thai nationals via information and technology innovations. These include operating the Saranrom Radio Network that includes public radio and internet radio; facilitating the undertaking and operation of foreign radio stations in Thailand; and working with other domestic stakeholders.

In 2018, the Thai government announced the implementation of the 20-year National Strategy, with the goal of becoming a developed country by 2037. Following that, the Ministry of Foreign Affairs formulated the 5S strategies of Security, Sustainability, Standard, Status and Synergy. The promotion of soft power and public diplomacy is included in the Status category. There are five core policy actions recommended under this plan: (1) increase the value of Thai brand and Thai popularity via art, culture and creative wisdom; (2) improve mutual understanding by enhancing multi-level cooperation with multi-stakeholders; (3) promote development and academic cooperation; (4) enhance national capacity as the hub of MICE; and (5) support Thai nationals to work at international organisations.

Although Thailand is rich in cultural and policy assets, it needs to cultivate more messengers and networks to promote and represent the country in the international arena. The Ministry has reactivated the Thailand Foundation, which was set up in 2007 to engage with foreign publics and enhance its national image by communicating Thai core values.

In the 2020s, public diplomacy will be more critical than ever to foreign policy as countries, particularly the small and medium nations in Southeast Asia, have witnessed intensifying geopolitical competition among the major powers. The trade war between the United States and China has expanded to technological competition, and their different values could well lead to an ideological clash. Moreover, the digitalisation of public diplomacy opens new communication channels that enable anyone to use social media to either support or challenge the government. At the same time, it could also turn social media into a space of contention. Therefore, it is time for the government to be proactive in engaging different strategic stakeholders.

To sum up, Thai public diplomacy has three main features. First, it targets both foreigners and Thai nationals. Second, it emphasises an informative communication style, rather than influencing foreign publics. Finally, the changing international and domestic environments determine the principle and practice of public diplomacy. Ultimately, the success of

Thailand's public diplomacy will hinge on how the country manages its relationship with different strategic stakeholders.

Seksan Anantasirikiat

Seksan Anantasirikiat is a Researcher at the International Studies Center, Ministry of Foreign Affairs in Thailand. He also served as the coordinator, ASEAN Roundtable, Seoul National University and a senior editor of the Seoul National University Journal of International Affairs.

References

Chantana, C. (2001). *The Role of Foreign Cultural Diplomats in Thailand and the Conduct of Thai Cultural Diplomacy Abroad (in Thai)*. Phitsanulok: Faculty of Education.

PR Thai Government. (2020). Thailand Ranks First in the Global COVID-19 Recovery Index. *Thailand Business News*, July 29. https://www.thailand-business-news.com/health/80125-thailand-ranks-first-in-the-global-covid-19-recovery-index.html

Supamit, P. (2017). การทูตสาธารณะของไทย กับแนวพระราชดำริของพระบาทสมเด็จพระเจ้าอยู่หัวรัชกาลท 9 [Thailand's Public Diplomacy and the King Rama 9's Royal Idea]. *Way Magazine*, October 24. https://waymagazine.org/public_diplomacy_king_bhumibol/

"Timeline of the Saranrom Radio," Unpublished document, Ministry of Foreign Affairs.

Vietnam

"*Public diplomacy has gained popularity among ASEAN members, with cultural diplomacy playing a central role. Culture is considered the best bridge between peoples and a strong facilitator for political and economic objectives – or national interests. This is even more so when political values are incompatible.*"

Thien Mu Pagoda, Hue

Unity in Diversity: Vietnam's Public Diplomacy in the ASEAN Context

Vu Lam

While the concept of public diplomacy is a 20th century product, the practice of influencing foreign publics could be traced back millennia. The practice certainly has never been foreign to former Southeast Asian kingdoms and polities or the Association of Southeast Asian Nations' (ASEAN) members. After all, cultural exchange and psychological warfare have been part of public outreach for centuries.

Today, new understandings of public diplomacy, no matter how diverse, share two conclusions: that public diplomacy must go past the point of one-way messaging and that the public(s) are not merely on the receiving end (Melissen, 2005). The main driving force behind these realities is the thriving information and communication technology (ICT) sector, which brings about two enormous implications.

First, there are few boundaries between the domestic and the international, as communication technologies have virtually flattened all the barriers. The more digitally literate people are, the more interconnected and influential the public becomes. Reaching out to netizen communities poses serious challenges and opportunities for the work of public diplomacy. In the broadest of terms, modern diplomacy is public diplomacy since there is no escaping from the public eye. In other words, public diplomacy is intermestic (La Porte, 2012), in the sense that it must address the people at home and abroad.

Second, the exponential production of information has shortened attention spans tremendously. Ironically, while the modern era allows the convenience of fact-checking at one's fingertip, it has also witnessed how both information and misinformation barely register and cannot wield long-term influence without serious attempts at relationship-building (Nye, 2019). As a result, today's public diplomacy is at its best when it aims to build mutual understanding and trust. The modern public diplomacy process, as such, cannot treat the general public as a passive audience. Non-state actors can take on a more active role, sometimes at the cost of state actors.

Evolving Public Diplomacy: From Propagandist to Participatory
The Vietnamese case is a prime example of the shift from traditional understandings to contemporary adaptations of public diplomacy. There is a slow transition from strategic objectives to more inclusive and long-term goals.

Before the penetration of ICTs, Vietnam adopted a strategic form of public diplomacy that aimed to win the hearts and minds of targeted foreign audiences. The party-state tailored messages, sent out delegates and conducted various exchanges with its international friends and foes.

External propaganda and people's diplomacy played an important role in the effective psychological warfare against the communist state's most powerful adversaries in the 20th century (Mehta, 2009). All the public diplomacy instruments were designed for high-impact and immediate effect to support the military front.

The domestic public, at the time, was secondary to the work of public diplomacy. They were, however, under the purview of a domestic form of propaganda, with manipulative messages that fostered nationalism and loyalty to communism. These two themes were often considered inseparable: patriotism means loving the socialist state.

The only meaningful bridge between the international and the domestic publics was the press, but it was not possible as the press has always been controlled by the state. Without any alternative channel, there was no real connection between the two realms. As such, the geographical divide resulted in the diminutive role of the domestic public in Vietnam's politics, which dissuaded the need for domestic outreach by the state. If anything, the press promoted the state's international triumphs to the domestic public to affirm the regime's political legitimacy.

After the Vietnam War, the country spiralled into a deep socio-economic recession due to various domestic and international headwinds. Inspired by the political and economic reform known as Doi Moi in 1986, ICTs, especially the internet, played a key role in Vietnam's global integration in the 1990s. Since then, ICTs have rapidly expanded the communication channels between Vietnam and the world. Along the way, online communities of Vietnamese at home and overseas have burgeoned. International audiences also have easier access to Vietnam's social life.

Vietnam's public diplomacy has now taken a turn towards inclusiveness and long-term visions. The main reason is that thanks to ICTs, public opinion has gained more traction in the regime's policymaking process. The contemporary, intertwined publics, including the domestic Vietnamese, the diaspora and international watchers, can influence Vietnam's global image and forestall its nation branding efforts.

The masses can be both a powerful advocate of and a major opponent to any official diplomatic endeavour. For instance, in 2014, Vietnam's government had to withdraw as host of the 2019 Asian Games – an event with diplomatic significance – due to unusually strong public objections (VnExpress, 2014). Similarly, Vietnam's tight grip on public participation has not gone unnoticed. The frequent crackdowns on political dissidents, and by extension, Vietnam's human rights record, have drawn flak from international critics of the communist regime.

At the same time, changes to Vietnam's foreign policy, including its revamped public diplomacy, have been applauded. For the past few decades, Vietnam has extended the olive branch to old enemies and nations with opposite political views, and actively engaged in multilateral mechanisms for global issues.

Vietnam's membership with ASEAN is the epitome of multilateralism, given the wide diversity and complexity of the regional setting. Apart from government-to-government diplomacy, Vietnam has also deployed various instruments of public diplomacy towards regional audiences, fostering a sense of collective identity among ASEAN peoples, as per ASEAN Community Vision 2025.

It is worth pointing out that public diplomacy is not the panacea for international relations, but rather part of a package solution that includes various levels of communication between nations. Multilateralism makes perfect sense for Vietnam. Wedged between major powers, especially China, Vietnam has little choice but to rely on multilateral institutions as a balancing act. Besides, aligning with foreign publics provides Vietnam with a powerful leverage for its political and economic objectives. Isolationism in the age of globalisation is undesirable and detrimental to a middle-income country whose exports play a major role in the economy.

Cultural Diplomacy: More Accessible and Acceptable
The complexity of the modern public requires a different approach from the Cold War era. Messages that are purely propagandist do not last long. Relations require mutual appreciation and understanding. In practice, one-way messaging must be accompanied by longer-term initiatives that go beyond the first impression. The new public diplomacy builds on the old one, embracing traditional and innovative instruments. Generally speaking, manipulation and coercion are antithetical to genuine and sustainable relations.

Vietnam, as such, has started to invest in cultural diplomacy as a key component of its foreign policy. The year 2009 marked the start of cultural diplomacy, and a national strategy was issued in 2011, all of which makes cultural diplomacy the linchpin of Vietnam's public diplomacy – to borrow an expression by the US State Department

(Advisory Committee on Cultural Diplomacy, 2005). Various activities have taken place, such as information campaigns on international and social media, cultural exchanges with ASEAN and other important partners, and cultural and language programmes for Vietnamese overseas.

While the main target is the foreign public, Vietnam has also realised the growing importance of gaining support from the domestic public and the Vietnamese diaspora. The four million Vietnamese overseas have stepped up their impact on Vietnam's politics with significant contributions to the economy. In the face of political discordance, the Vietnam government appeals to Vietnamese communities by forging a collective sense of culturalist national identity. In other words, the regime leverages nationalism to serve its interests, and the best way to do so is to promote cultural diplomacy at home and abroad. In this process, non-state actors have been increasingly active in Vietnam's cultural exchanges, either as sponsor, collaborator or messenger.

The culture element is the common denominator between Vietnam and many ASEAN nations. Cultural diplomacy has also been promoted by other ASEAN members, including Indonesia, Malaysia, Singapore and Cambodia. The ASEAN Secretariat, too, encourages cultural relations among ASEAN peoples under the framework of ASEAN Community Vision 2025. The rationale behind this region's eager adoption of cultural diplomacy is multifaceted and this essay does not allow for a deep analysis. But there are several obvious reasons.

First, Southeast Asia is among the most culturally and ethnically diverse regions. As such, there is a strong consensus among ASEAN governments that the culture element is crucial to their soft power arsenals (Hall & Smith, 2013). Cultural initiatives can enrich mutual understanding, dialogue and sustainable relations inwards and outwards. Culture is also more accessible and acceptable to the general public than political undertakings. This is especially so as the political values of many ASEAN members are not compatible with the Western world.

There is also a strong economic incentive to implement cultural diplomacy. Cultural appeal is crucial to nation branding, which in turn greatly benefits tourism (Ang et al., 2015). International arrivals play a significant role among regional economies. As of 2018, regional countries attracted about 135 million visitors intra- and extra-ASEAN, with the biggest beneficiaries being Thailand, Indonesia, Singapore, Malaysia and Vietnam (ASEANstats, 2020). As such, cultural diplomacy appears to yield high returns on investments.

In summary, public diplomacy has gained popularity among ASEAN members, with cultural diplomacy playing a central role. Culture is considered the best bridge between peoples and a strong facilitator for political and economic objectives – or national interests. This is even more so when political values are incompatible.

Vietnam, despite its tumultuous past and atypical political system, has eagerly adopted culture-based public diplomacy. The technology-infused public sphere also prompts a gradual transition from one-way messaging to dialogue and relationship-building. As a result, Vietnam's public diplomacy today is more inclusive and participatory than propagandist and manipulative. This rings true for many ASEAN members as well, proving that there is commonality in diversity.

Vu Lam

Vu Lam is currently a visiting fellow at the Australian National University. He holds a PhD in international and political studies from the University of New South Wales and a Master of International Studies (Advanced) from the University of Queensland, Australia. His areas of interest include soft power, public diplomacy, and the application of social constructivism on non-Western actors in international politics.

References

Advisory Committee on Cultural Diplomacy. *Cultural Diplomacy: The Linchpin of Public Diplomacy*. US: US Department of State, 2005. https://www.state.gov/cultural-diplomacy-the-linchpin-of-public-diplomacy/

Ang, Ien, Yudhishthir Raj Isar, and Phillip Mar. "Cultural diplomacy: beyond the national interest?". *International Journal of Cultural Policy 21*, no. 4 (2015): 365-81.

ASEANstats. ASEAN Visitor Arrivals Dashboard. https://data.aseanstats.org/dashboard/tourism.

Hall, Ian, and Frank Smith. "The Struggle for Soft Power in Asia: Public Diplomacy and Regional Competition." *Asian Security 9*, no. 1 (2013): 1-18.

La Porte, Teresa. "The Impact of 'Intermestic' Non-State Actors on the Conceptual Framework of Public Diplomacy." *The Hague Journal of Diplomacy 7*, no. 4 (2012): 441-58.

Mehta, Harish C. "People's Diplomacy": The Diplomatic Front of North Vietnam During the War Against the United States, 1965-1972." 2009.

Melissen, Jan. "The New Public Diplomacy: Between Theory and Practice." *The New Public Diplomacy: Soft Power in International Relations*, edited by Jan Melissen, 4-27. Basingstoke [UK]; New York: Palgrave Macmillan, 2005.

Afterword

"*All of us need to better understand the science of how people think, feel and act in different situations and contexts. When we apply these insights to practical issues involving trust, perspective taking and cultural differences, we will function more effectively in our international interactions to strengthen people-to-people relations across borders and build global communities.*"

David Chan

David Chan is a Professor of Psychology and Director of Behavioural Sciences Institute at the Singapore Management University. His works, published in top psychology, management and methods journals, have been cited over 12,000 times in various disciplines. In this piece, he offers his take on the psychology of international interactions in strengthening people-to-people relations.

The Psychology of International Interactions and People-to-People Relations

In our interconnected world, there are two pragmatic principles that are critical for nations – big or small – to survive and thrive. One is upholding the international rule of law. The other is building strong international relations, trust and friendships at all levels and across all sectors. This cross-country and cross-cultural relationship building is not just between governments, but also between individuals, groups and organisations. Indeed, making friends and strengthening people-to-people relations across borders build global communities. It lays the foundation for constructive collaboration and co-creation of solutions to enhance individual and societal well-being, and progress towards a better world.

But people interactions are not always positive, especially when individuals, groups or countries differ in their immediate goals, interests and even values. How then do we enable positive attitudes and experiences in interactions and strengthen people-to-people relations?

Let me offer three distinct but related suggestions: First, we need to better understand the psychology of trust and appreciate its fragility and power. Second, to build trust and quality relationships with others, we must understand what others are thinking and learn to see things from their perspectives. Third, in an era of disagreements and disputes arising from diverse and disparate perspectives, we must understand cultural differences and also recognise commonalities and complementarities amid differences to prevent the negative and promote the positive.

The Psychology of Trust

When trust is low, people-to-people interaction is not constructive and effective functioning is hampered. When individuals do not believe what others say and do, it is difficult to discuss issues, identify problems, create solutions, implement a new initiative as intended, change a prior decision, explain an error or galvanise people to help manage a situation.

Of course, with power, one may still get people to do something without their willing cooperation. But it will not be sustained and sustainable when people do it only because they have to, rather than because they want to and believe they ought to. It may even backfire. People can obey on the surface but do the opposite privately or retaliate in various ways.

Trust is difficult to build, easily eroded and difficult to restore once lost. The good news is, from research and practice, much is now known about the different aspects of trust and how the trust process works. This basic knowledge, together with understanding how humans think, feel and act in the contexts of the issues that people care about, can help us prevent trust erosion, repair trust violation and enhance trust development.

Trust perceptions matter a lot. A person may be objectively trustworthy on an issue based on his or her competence and character. But if contextual factors have negatively affected trust perception, then there will still be low trust. For example, others may distrust a person because they lack access to relevant facts about the issues involved. Alternatively, they may have misinterpreted certain facts or have been misled to believe that some falsehoods or inaccuracies are factually true. Or a failure in coordination or communication may have confounded issues and led to negative trust perceptions. So what matters in trust is perception — the trustee's trustworthiness as perceived by the trustor, which is based on what the trustor thinks of the trustee's competence, integrity and benevolence.

Trust in competence refers to people's perception of the person's ability to solve problems and effectively address their concerns. Trust in integrity has to do with the perception of the person's character including issues of honesty, incorruptibility and impartiality. Trust in benevolence refers to people's confidence that the person is authentic (saying what he means and meaning what he says) and has good intentions or motivations when making a decision or undertaking a particular action.

Trust in benevolence is one of the hardest forms of trust to gain. It is one that means a lot to people, but is often neglected by the person seeking to be trusted. Often, the problem may not be that the person is insincere, but that he is not perceived as sincere because he has not paid adequate attention to the nature of his actions, engagement and communications. Trust in benevolence increases when people believe that the person's action is intended to serve their interests and is motivated by genuine concern for their well-being, rather than personal vested interests. It gets eroded when people think that decisions and actions affecting them are made without empathising with their concerns and needs.

To build a high-trust climate, we need to understand better how humans think, feel and act in the context of the issues that people care about. Whoever we are, it is important to have the humility, learning orientation and objectivity to draw lessons on trust from people's responses and experiences, both positive and negative. This brings us to the important issue of perspective-taking to enhance positive interactions and strengthen relations.

Seeing Things from Different Perspectives

One of the most critical aspects of constructive interactions and working together is learning to see things from another's perspective, by which I mean to consider how things appear to the other party. Perspective-taking requires constant reminders to ourselves and proactive effort because it is human tendency to see things from our own viewpoint only rather than from another's perspective.

Even when everyone is presented with the same facts, they can have different meanings when seen from different perspectives. The perspective each person adopts influences what is considered central or peripheral, obvious or obscure, and even present or absent – just like how the view of our living room and the things in it can look very different depending on where we stand. If we do not understand a person's perspective, what is very meaningful and sensible to the person may look absurd to us. But if we are going through the same situation as the person, we may behave just like the person did, and think it is perfectly normal or the right thing to do.

Studies in the behavioural sciences have shown that we do not see things as they are. We see things as we are. We make interpretations according to our beliefs and past experiences about ourselves and others. We give meanings to things in the context of the circumstances we live or find ourselves in, including how we are affected by the events or situation. Moreover, once we have adopted a perspective, it is difficult to suspend or change it. It is even harder to take another's perspective that is different from ours. This is mainly due to the human tendency of confirmatory bias – we are predisposed to see what we expect to see. We seek out and interpret information in a way that will likely confirm our perspective.

So we need to recognise that some of the differences in viewpoints between ourselves, or between ourselves and foreigners or international communities, are probably in part due to the differences in life experiences. We cannot live the foreigner's or the international community's life experiences. But if we all take some time to put ourselves in their shoes before we advocate a position or react to differing views, it will be more likely that we can move forward constructively even if disagreements still occur.

If we can see things differently, from another person's perspective, we can have fewer strong disagreements and more constructive responses to contentious issues when working together. At the minimum, we will be more careful in what we say or do in a difficult situation to avoid escalating the negatives. On many complex issues involving international interactions, can we suspend or get outside our own perspective and try to see things from another's perspective? If we can and when we do so, we may find our own perspective not as valid as we thought. Or, at least, realise that it is not the only valid one. Of course, we may still hold on to our perspective for good reasons. But we are now able to address the differences better because we understand the other perspective.

Interacting internationally and working together in global communities is not just about contributing our resources and expressing our perspectives. If we learn to see things from another's perspective and apply it adequately, we are more likely to prevent misunderstandings, enable constructive conversations and achieve win-win solutions among the stakeholders. Most importantly, perspective-taking will advance our mutual interests and achieve our common goals, ultimately addressing problems and benefiting those whom we are trying to help.

So, in the face of differences and disagreements, it is good to pause, take a deep breath and reflect before reacting. When we see things from another's perspective, we will react in a more effective manner and it is more likely that we can reduce negativity, increase positivity and co-create solutions.

Cultural Differences and Sensitivity

Finally, a critical enabler of positive attitudes and experiences in international interactions to strengthen people-to-people relations is to be culturally sensitive to the thoughts, feelings and actions of others who are different from us. To be culturally sensitive, the first step is simply to have some basic knowledge or awareness of the way of life, societal norms and modes of thinking associated with the particular culture that is different from our own. It is also about being interested in and informed about major regional and global issues and keeping abreast of how the relevant culture or country may be affected by these issues and developments.

Cultural sensitivity requires understanding of cultural differences, but it also involves being aware of our own cultural perspectives and biases. This relates back to the above points about guarding against our confirmatory bias tendencies and learning to see things from diverse perspectives different from our own.

Also, cultural sensitivity is not just about learning to be tolerant of differences. The essence of it is about understanding what the differences are, why they exist and how to manage them in a cross-cultural interaction. The differences need not be a liability. They can be an asset when the diversity complements each other. So cultural sensitivity is about both preventing bad outcomes and promoting good outcomes.

Dealing with cultural differences should be construed as an important aspect of global citizenship, which means it involves going beyond differences to focus on commonalities. To be a global citizen is to be human – to recognise that amid cultural differences and diversity across nationalities, we all belong to the same human race. This involves respecting human dignity and rights, and caring for and helping each other, regardless of geography, passports and skin colour. It also means recognising that we inhabit the same planet, and with it comes the responsibility to do our part to protect the environment.

We must understand cultural differences to prevent unintended negative consequences and promote harmony, while recognising that our commonalities and complementarities amid differences can foster collaboration, respect for human dignity and social responsibility to enhance individual and societal well-being.

In sum, all of us need to better understand the science of how people think, feel and act in different situations and contexts. When we apply these insights to practical issues involving trust, perspective-taking and cultural differences, we will function more effectively in our international interactions to strengthen people-to-people relations across borders and build global communities.

www.ingramcontent.com/pod-product-compliance
Lightning Source LLC
Chambersburg PA
CBHW070342100426
42812CB00005B/1400

* 9 7 8 9 8 1 1 2 5 0 4 3 9 *